Chinese Poetic Closure

Asian Thought and Culture

Charles Wei-hsun Fu
General Editor

Vol. 10

PETER LANG
New York • Washington, D.C./Baltimore
Bern • Frankfurt am Main • Berlin • Vienna • Paris

Yang Ye

Chinese Poetic Closure

PETER LANG
New York • Washington, D.C./Baltimore
Bern • Frankfurt am Main • Berlin • Vienna • Paris

Library of Congress Cataloging-in-Publication Data

Ye, Yang.
Chinese poetic closure / Yang Ye.
p. cm. — (Asian thought and culture; vol. 10)
Includes bibliographical references and index.
1. Chinese poetry—History and criticism. 2. Chinese literature—History and criticism. 3. Poetics. I. Title. II. Series.
PL2307.Y35 895.1'1009—dc20 95-41558
ISBN 978-0-8204-3061-4
ISSN 0893-6870

Bibliographic information published by **Die Deutsche Nationalbibliothek**.
Die Deutsche Nationalbibliothek lists this publication in the "Deutsche Nationalbibliografie"; detailed bibliographic data are available on the Internet at http://dnb.d-nb.de/.

The paper in this book meets the guidelines for permanence and durability of the Committee on Production Guidelines for Book Longevity of the Council of Library Resources.

29 Broadway, 18th floor, New York, NY 10006
www.peterlang.com

Printed in the United States of America

To the memory of my father
Yeh Ts'ung-ch'i (1904–1984)

Contents

Acknowledgements

THIS book has taken quite a few years in the making. I am simply unable to list all the names of authors to whom I owe an intellectual debt as they are just too many, but I have tried to acknowledge their inspiration and help in my notes and bibliography. However, as the format of this note allows, I would still like to give my special thanks to the following.

The core of the book's theme first took shape in an oral presentation that I gave to a meeting of the East Coast Chinese Poetry Group on a spring afternoon in 1987, at Yale University, and even today I still recall with gratitude the constructive comments and warm encouragement I received from all the "patricians," peers, and friends in the audience that day.

The next reincarnation of the book took shape in my doctoral dissertation at Harvard University in 1989, which owed its completion to the guidance and support of many. I want to thank first of all Professor Stephen Owen, who devoted much of his precious time to reading my manuscript and making invaluable suggestions. His erudite knowledge of and spectacular insight into Chinese poetry has been, then and now, a constant source of inspiration ever since I became his student a decade ago. I am also very grateful to Professor Helen Vendler, to whose superb art of reading poetry I have tried to "play the sedulous ape" (to borrow the expression of Robert Louis Stevenson) in my own clumsy practice. I should also mention here that it was actually at her suggestion to include a topic on poetic structure in my general examinations that engaged my interest in poetic closure and in Barbara Herrstein Smith's path-finding study. I want to thank Professor Per Nykrog for sharing his intelligence and wit with me in reading French poetry. To all my other teachers at Harvard I owe a lifelong debt as well, but I would like to mention in particular Professors Patrick Hanan and Jurij Striedter. The former exemplifies the solid and thorough scholarship of Chinese studies in the West, and has offered me help and support in many and various ways; and the latter first opened my eyes to the illumination of Russian Formalism. Professor Daniel Aaron was my earliest linkage to Harvard. I attended his lecture on American literature when I was still an undergraduate at Fudan University in Shanghai. Ever since I arrived in Cambridge, he has been a mentor and a dear friend to me.

Over the years, in the process of revising my manuscript after I assumed my teaching position, somewhat in the style of the traditional Chinese landscape painter, "five days for a stream and ten for a rock," I have benefitted from the encouragement and support of my colleagues at the University of California, Riverside. Professor Irving Yucheng Lo of Indiana University, a long-time family friend, read the entire manuscript, and made many perceptive suggestions. I would also like to thank the Editor of the series of *Asian Thoughts and Culture*, Professor Charles Wei-hsun Fu, for his glowing review of the book and his recommendation to include the book in the series.

I would also like to thank my wife, Cora Ha, for undergoing the long process of tempering through various stages of completing this book. With love and nostalgia, I recall the good old days of learning to chant and interpret Chinese poetry under my father's tutoring, the sheer pleasure of which I still try my best to introduce to my students today. For all the remaining errors and imperfections in the book I am solely responsible.

Y.Y.

Table of Chinese Historical Dynasties

Chou (Period of Springs and Autumns)	770–476 B.C.
Period of Warring States	475–221 B.C.
Ch'in	221–206 B.C.
Han	
Western Han	206 B.C.–A.D. 8
Hsin (Interregnum)	9–24
Eastern Han	25–220
Three Kingdoms	220–265
Chin (Western Chin)	266–316
Southern Dynasties	
Eastern Chin	317–420
Sung	420–479
Ch'i	479–502
Liang	502–557
Ch'en	557–589
Sui	589–618
T'ang	618–907
Period of Five Dynasties and Ten Kingdoms	907–960
Sung	960–1279
Yüan (Mongol)	1279–1368
Ming	1368–1644
Ch'ing (Manchu)	1644–1911

Note on Transliteration of Chinese Characters

FOR the transliteration of Chinese names and words, I have in general followed the Wade-Giles system, with the only modification in the use of *yi* instead of *i*. Exceptions are made in the case of names that have been in use for a long time and may sound more familiar to Western readers, such as the Latinized names Confucius and Mencius, the *I-ching* (*Book of Changes*), Li Po (rather than Li Pai), and some geographic names.

1

Introduction

Poetic Structure and Poetic Text

A study of poetic *closure* is primarily a study of the *structure* of a poetic *text*. The English word *structure*, like its equivalents in European languages (the French *la structure* and the German *die Struktur*), has derived from the Latin word *struere*, i.e., *to construct* or *to put things in order*. Likewise the English word *text* shares its origin with the word *texture* in the Latin participle *textum*, which means "that which is woven." Understood in this sense, what we discuss as *poetic structure* here includes the different means of *constructing* or *weaving* a poetic text. Obviously, the structure of a poetic text involves many and various elements or units of the text. As a literary term, however, the word *structure* has more frequently been used as an equivalent for *prosody*, which as a matter of fact is only one of the many aspects of that construction.

A basic concept of the Russian Formalist critics can help further elucidate the use of the term *structure* in this study. In his extensive discussion of plot construction, Viktor Sklovskij has formulated the distinction between *fabula* and *sjuzet*: the former refers to the raw material of a story, i.e., its basic causal-temporal relationship; and the latter, the arrangement and presentation of that basic stuff at the hand of the author.[1]

Although Sklovskij's discussion was originally made in the context of narrative prose, the concept of *fabula* and *sjuzet* has been applied to literary composition in general with some variation. In the light of this concept, the study of poetic structure may also be understood as the study of the *sjuzet* in its manipulation and presentation of the *fabula*, which may be illustrated by the following comparison of two texts (*sjuzet*) based on a similar subject or origin (*fabula*). Dorothy Wordsworth's journal recorded that on Thursday, April 15, 1802, she and her brother William, the poet, took a walk along the Lake, during which they saw some daffodils. She wrote as follows:

> It was a threatening, misty morning, but mild. We set off after dinner from Eusemere, ... The wind was furious, ... The wind seized our breath. The Lake was rough, ... When we were in the woods beyond Gowbarrow Park we saw a few daffodils close to the water-side. We fancied that the lake had floated the seeds ashore, and that the little colony had so sprung up. But as we went along there were more and yet more; and at last, under the boughs of the trees, we saw that there was a long belt of them along the shore, about the breadth of a country turnpike road. I never saw daffodils so beautiful. They grew among the mossy stones about and about them; some rested their heads upon these stones as on a pillow for weariness; and the rest *tossed* and reeled and *danced*, and seemed as if they verily laughed with the wind, that flew upon them over the Lake; they looked so *gay*, ever *glancing*, ever changing.[2]

Two years later, under her brother's pen, however, the trip was transformed into the poet's solitary walk:

> I wandered lonely as a cloud
> That floats on high o'er vales and hills,
> When all at once I saw a crowd,
> A host, of golden daffodils;
> Beside the lake, beneath the trees,
> Fluttering and dancing in the breeze.
>
> Continuous as the stars that shine
> And twinkle on the milky way,
> They stretched in never-ending line
> Along the margin of a bay:
> Ten thousand saw I at a glance,
> Tossing their heads in sprightly dance.
>
> The waves beside them danced, but they
> Outdid the sparkling waves in glee;
> A poet could not but be gay,
> In such a jocund company;
> I gazed—and gazed—but little thought
> What wealth the show to me had brought:
>
> For oft, when on my couch I lie
> In vain or in pensive mood,
> They flash upon that inward eye
> Which is the bliss of solitude;
> And then my heart with pleasure fills,

And dances with the daffodils.

Placed side by side, the two texts show quite a few differences in addition to that between prose and poetry, even though they obviously have derived from the same occasion. The poet kept in the poem some of his sister's wording (those italicized in Dorothy's text), but he also made a few important changes during his own writing process, his "recollection in tranquility." Besides excluding his walking companion entirely from the scene, he also substituted a *breeze* for what Dorothy had described as a *furious* wind that "seized [their] breath," a change which corresponds well to the overall milieu of beauty and harmony in his poem. From the generic features of the diary as a form of composition, we may consider Dorothy's record as a more truthful account of the actual event, the trip that they made together that day. What is presented at the opening of William's poem, on the other hand, is obviously quite a different account of the event, even a *distortion*. A poet, nevertheless, has the *poetic license* to manipulate his *fabula*. It does not need the genius of a William Wordsworth to sense that it is much more poetic to say "I wandered lonely as a cloud" than, for instance, "We strolled together as clouds." To appreciate the wonderful opening of this poem in terms of the relation between that literary event (*fabula*), probably more truthfully recorded in Dorothy's diary, which her brother had read before his composition of the poem, and the way the poet presented it (*sjuzet*), is to read the poem in terms of its *structure*.

Under the category of *poetic structure*, one may place such structural units as poetic titles, beginnings, endings, and last but by no means the least, the structural patterns in their relations with each of these separate units and with the entire text.

Now one may argue that just as a thousand people have a thousand faces, each poetic text has its own individual features which, according to an argument prevalent since the New Critics, have to be dealt with individually; hence it is perhaps meaningless to have a general study of any of its structural units. Such an argument, however, is to be taken with a grain of salt. While it is desirable to study every poem in its own right, real appreciation of literature comes from comparison and contrast. Just as the thousand faces can be distinguished according to, say, complexion or shape, poems can be studied in groups of, for instance, genre, period, school, or structure. The same is true of their structural units. Categorization is inherent in human nature, even though one certainly has to keep in mind that it is not, and should not be, an end in itself. Also, what has made the issue relevant to our discussion is the realization that the categoric features are most often inherent in the text itself, and are not mere functions of the motives of the categorizer.

A poetic text may be regarded as a system not all the components of which interact equally. Most often it is one in which, in the creative process of the *sjuzet*'s manipulation of the *fabula*, some components are projected into the foreground and become *dominant*, to use another Formalist term, while some others recede into the background or even become absent in the text. The *dominant*, in the words of Roman Jacobson, is the *foregrounding* of one or a group of elements. It is the focusing component of a work of art that rules, determines, and transforms the other components. It is largely through the *dominant* that a poetic text takes on its specific features. Although the *dominant* parts do not stand entirely on their own, they do not function merely as constituents of the whole either, but actually in their turn have their own important structural functions, and often their *dominance*, in the whole text. Largely in the sense of literary history, Jacobson used the term *dominant* to refer to parts of poetic structure (such as rhyme, syllabic scheme, and intonational unity), or to different genres of art (such as visual arts, music, and verbal art). To Jacobson, the *dominant* does not remain the same all the time, but rather shifts from age to age. The shifting of the *dominant* underscores the tension between canon and artistic novelty, the latter being understood as a deviation from the former which often gives shape to a new canon.[3]

Attention to Poetic Structure in Chinese Critical Tradition

Since early times Chinese writers and critics have paid much attention to poetic structure as well as to the importance of structural units. An emphasis on the importance of parts in their relation to the whole may have had its origin in the critique of the practical use of literature, such as during the "Period of Spring and Autumn" (the 8th to the 5th century B.C.), when texts from the ancient anthology of songs, the *Shih-ching* (*Book of Songs*), were widely used and quoted for political, diplomatic, and various social functions. Lines were frequently garbled out of context—what the T'ang classical scholar K'ung Ying-ta called *tuan chang ch'ü yi*, "interpreting a passage out of its context."[4] In this way, many poems in the *Shih-ching* became widely known through frequent citations, and were transmitted, so to speak, "on everyone's lips."

The earliest Chinese writer known to have attributed great importance to separate parts in a literary text was the Chin poet Lu Chi. His *Wen-fu* (*The Rhyme-prose Exposition on Literature*) is primarily a detailed description of the writing process. In talking about the essentials of literary expression he suggested the concept of *ching-ch'e* ("cracking horsewhip"):

> Set a piece of expression at a key position
> To make a cracking horse-whip for the entire text.

What is meant here, according to traditional exegesis, is that in a literary composition, it is desirable to put down a word or phrase at an appropriate place which, though incomplete in itself, may become a point of convergence, and which may function like a "cracking horse-whip" to invigorate the whole piece. The term *ching-ch'e* has since been used to refer to words, phrases, sentences and other structural units which play an important role in the text: units that spur and alert the reader's attention, as the original meaning of that equestrian term suggests. This approximates to the Formalist idea of the *dominant* when applied to parts of poetic structure, though Lu Chi's original use of the term seems to have put the emphasis more specifically on the smaller units of words and phrases.[5]

Liu Hsieh's *Wen-hsin tiao-lung* (*Carving Dragon at the Heart of Literature*), written circa. 502, is the earliest systematically organized book of Chinese literary criticism. Several of its fifty chapters touch upon the topic of poetic structure, but most notably in the chapters "Stanza and Line" (*Chang-chü*) and "Fluency and Coherence" (*Fu-hui*). These two chapters examine the structure of a literary text, especially how the parts work towards the unity of the text. They investigate the relation between the subject and the art, between the material that provides the basis for literary composition and its arrangement under the author's pen. The latter chapter also contains some comments on beginning and closure, and on their significance in relation to the entire text, which is to be further discussed in detail later in this study.[6]

Such a close attention to parts as the organizing and animating center of the whole had also been found in the comments on art made by the great Chin dynasty painter Ku K'ai-chih, who asserted the paramount importance of painting the eyes in portraits. When asked why he usually would not add the eyes to his figures until years after he finished all the rest of a portrait, Ku remarked that in a portrait, the four limbs and the body were less important than what he called "those things" (*e-tu*), i.e., the eyeballs which conveyed the spirit and reflected the real image of the person.[7] Later, the term *yen* or *mu* ("eye") was sometimes used by critics to refer to poetic units. A book of prosody attributed to the T'ang poet Chia Tao, *The Secret Purports of the Two "Southern" Sections* (*Erh-nan mi-chih*), defines the Chinese term for "title" (*t'i-mu*) literally as the "theme and eyes" of the poet.[8] The Sung literary critics further developed a concept of the *shih yen* ("the poetic eye(s)"), which in their terminology stand for key words in the lines, not unlike Liu Hsieh's "cracking horsewhip." Yen Yü, a thirteenth century critic, identified the three points that demand skillful handling (*yung-kung*) in the composition of poetry, namely, *ch'i chieh*, beginning and closure; *chü-fa*, the structure of the lines; and *tzu-yen*, the "eye" of words (the choice of *le mot juste*, usually a word denoting a movement or a descriptive word, at a specified position within a line). As Stephen Owen has pointed out, all three points were common topics of Chinese technical criticism.[9]

Towards the end of the Six Dynasties Period (6th century), there was already a growing technical concern for prosody. The poet Shen Yüeh first advocated the theory of the "Four Tones" (*ssu-sheng*) and the "Eight Defects" (*pa-ping*) which, as the modern scholar Hu Shih suggested, was perhaps inspired by the introduction of the Sanskrit practice of chanting Buddhist sutra texts.[10] The technical concern was instrumental to the formation of the *lü-shih* (regulated verse) in Early T'ang. Exactly because of the rise of the new form, and partially also due to the inclusion of poetry-writing in the T'ang civil service examinations, there appeared a number of prosody handbooks which often included collections of paradigmatic poetic lines. Some of such handbooks still exist today in *The Secret Book of Literary Mirror* (*Wen-ching mi-fu-lun* or *Bunkyo hifuron* in its Japanese title), compiled by the Kōbō Daishi, the Japanese Buddhist monk who went to live in China for three years at the beginning of the ninth century. The wide use of such handbooks contributed to the individual significance of beginning and closure, as well as to other structural units of the *lü-shih* form. Incidentally, body terms were used for each of the four couplets of a *lü-shih* text: they are respectively called the *head*, the *chin*, the *neck*, and the *tail* couplet.

Starting in the Sung dynasty, probably originating from the pedagogical practice of private tutoring schools, which prospered in the period, a particular way of reading literary texts added to the attention to parts in criticism. The *ch'üan-tien* (circles and dots) method consisted of using the writing brush, or later a seal specially made for that purpose, to mark out favorite lines in classic texts with dots and small circles. The implementation of this reading method identified the "cracking horsewhip" and the "poetic eye" within a line, or more often the most commendable lines within a poem, and attached greater significance to individual parts of a literary text. From the numerous books of *shih-hua* ("Remarks on Poetry") in the Sung to, just to give one example, the *Shih-sou* (*A Poetic Assembly*), a book of poetry criticism by the Ming critic Hu Ying-ling, there were extensive discussions of individual lines and couplets.

All such attention to parts played a crucial role in giving rise to the critical concern (sometimes the *meta-poetic* concern as in the works of poets themselves) with the craft of poetic beginning and closure in the Chinese tradition through the ages, a phenomenon unrivalled in Western poetry and poetics.

POETIC BEGINNING AND POETIC ENDING

As early as in the age of the ancient Greeks, Aristotle had already raised the issue of "beginning, middle, and end" in his *Poetics*, but he did not go into any detail on it. In fact the issue had never been thoroughly explored in the West until in Barbara Herrnstein Smith's pioneering study, *Poetic Closure: A Study of How Poems End* (1968). Exemplary as Smith's book is, its range of discussion is largely restricted to English and American poetry.

Although beginnings and closure have only occasionally and casually been the object of critical attention, some Western poets, through their own creative practice, have understood their significance. Byron remarked, in his *Don Juan*, that

> Nothing [is] so difficult as a beginning
> In poesy, unless perhaps the end.[11]

The American poet Henry Wadsworth Longfellow also noticed:

> Great is the art of beginning, but greater is the art of ending;
> Many a poem is marred by a superfluous verse.[12]

Like other structural units, the beginning and the ending often work in a way not unlike what Lu Chi had called "cracking horsewhip," that which plays a *dominant* role in the text. Among English poets, for example, John Donne often made use of forceful surprise beginnings:

> Goe, and catche a falling starre,
> Get with child a mandrake roote, ... (*Song*)

> Busie old foole, unruly Sunne, ... (*The Sun Rising*)

> For Godsake hold your tongue, and let me love, ... (*The Canonization*)

These openings, in the form of imperative sentences and apostrophes, create a dramatic tension that catches the reader's attention, and often curiosity as well, from the very start, in its unusual mode of address that seems to shove the reader immediately into a theater set for him, alluring, intriguing, puzzling. The reader is urged to listen with full attention, as in a theater, to the speaker in the poem as to a performer on the stage. And in many of Donne's poems with such openings, the reader will thenceforth be further bombarded by a series of unusual expressions and imagery. Donne, perhaps more than any English poet before him, integrated the art of drama into lyric poetry.[13]

In the Chinese tradition Ts'ao Chih, a major poet of the period of the "Three Kingdoms" (220–265), often employed forceful and unexpected beginnings in his poems, and has long been celebrated for his superb skills in the practice.[14] One often cited example of such skills is the opening of his valediction presented to a close friend and fellow poet Hsü Kan, who had lost favor in the court:

> A wind startled, whirling the white sun off,
> Suddenly, 'twas back to the western hills![15]

The opening is almost absurd in its hyperbolic description at first sight: it seems to have little connection with the rest of the text, basically words of encouragement for his disheartened friend. On a more careful look, however, the suddenness of the change from light to dark is allegorical: it sets the background for the poems's melancholy theme of departure, as the two friends are blown part by destiny as by a "startling wind," and their happy, carefree days of union are gone, just like the daylight receding its place to darkness.

There is also a kind of *dominant* opening that serves to define the context, using deictic terms of person, time, or space to set up a framework for the complete text. In the first of his sonnet series *Chimères*, entitled *El Desdichado*, the French poet Gérard de Nerval began with lines richly charged with allusions:

> Je suis le Ténébreux,—le Veuf,—l'Inconsolé,
> Le prince d'Aquitaine à la tour abolie:...
>
> [I am the shade, the widower, the unconsoled,
> The Aquitanian Prince in his wreck of a tower...][16]

Walt Whitman opened his *Song of Myself* in much the same way, though compared to Nerval his style is more succinct and straightforward:

> I celebrate myself, and sing myself,
> And what I assume you shall assume,
> For every atom belonging to me as good belongs to you.

Looking back upon Chinese poetry one may find a similarly self-defining beginning in a poem by the great Chinese poet Li Po:

> I was formerly that crazy man of Ch'u;
> Singing the song of phoenix, I jeered at K'ung Ch'iu.[17]

Here Li Po made an allusion to the story in the *Analects* about how Confucius was derided by a "maniac" of the Ch'u state during his travel. By identifying himself with "that crazy man," and by calling Confucius or "Master K'ung" (who by Li Po's age had long been sanctioned as the sage) by his name K'ung Ch'iu, directly and irreverently, the poet was deliberately displaying his own unorthodox disposition.

Each of the three texts above begins in what Chinese critics traditionally called the rhetoric of *k'ai meng chien shan*—"open the door and the mountain emerges right in sight." Such an opening frequently carries the sense of personal manifesto, and provides a framework, or in Chinese critical terminology, a *ku* ("bone"), for the entire text.

Endings could just as well become dominant in a similar way. Anyone who has read Villon's poetry, for example, would hardly ever forget the famous refrain of his *Ballade des dames du Temps jadis* (*Ballad of the Ladies of Bygone Days*):

> Mais où sont les neiges d'antan?
>
> [But where now is yesterday's snow?]

The use of the conjunction (*Mais*) at the beginning of the line suggests a pause and a switch: a pause for painful summarizing and recollection, a switch to highly metaphorical and lyrical imagery. The phrase *les neiges d'antan* crystallizes all the beauty, youthfulness and virginity of the celebrated ladies that he enumerated in the poem, ending it with a lingering echo that resounds in the reader's mind.

Mallarmé made a similarly marvelous use of the same conjunction at the end of his *Brise marine* (*Sea Breeze*), one of his earlier poems:

> La chair est triste, hélas! et j'ai lu tous les livres.
> Fuir! là-bas fuir! Je sens que des oiseaux sont ivres
> D'être parmi l'écume inconnue et les cieux!
> Rien, ni les vieux jardins reflétés par les yeux
> Ni retiendra ce coeur qui dans la mer se trempe
> Ô nuits! ni la clarté déserte de ma lampe
> Sur le vide papier que la blancheur défend,
> Et ni la jeune femme allaiotant son enfant.
> Je partirai! Steamer balançant ta mâture,
> Lève l'ancre pour une exotique nature!
> Un Ennui, désolé par les cruels espoirs,
> Croit encore à l'adieu suprême des mouchoirs!
> Et, peut-être, les mâts, invitant les orages
> Sont-ils de ceux qu'un vent penche sur les naufrages
> Perdus, sans mâts, sans mâts, ni fertiles îlots...
> Mais, ô mon coeur, entends le chant des matelots!
>
> [The flesh is sad, alas! and I've read all the books.
> Flee! flee afar! I feel that the birds are drunk
> To be between the unknown waves and the sky!
> Nothing—not old gardens reflected in our eyes—
> Will hold back this heart, which soaks itself in the sea
> Oh nights! nor the desolate light of my lamp
> Over the blank paper defended by its own whiteness,
> Nor the young wife feeding her child.
> I shall depart! A steamer, swinging its masts,

Weighs the anchor for an exotic Nature!
An ennui, sorrow-stricken with cruel hopes,
Still believes in the final farewell of handkerchiefs!
And, perhaps, the masts, inviting storms,
Are among those who in a wind bending over shipwrecks
Get lost, with no masts, no masts, nor fertile islands...
But, oh my heart, listen to the song of the sailors!]

The poem consists of eight couplets, but it is in one piece without any divisions. However, it moves through transitions as if from one stanza to another. The poet starts the poem by telling us how the speaker feels the boredom of his present life and how he longs for an escape. Then, in the first transition which takes place in line 5, he begins to enumerate things to be left behind, things that are common and seemingly trivial, but are nevertheless full of warmth and sweetness. With the second transition that arrives in line 9, he turns to an awesome description of storm and shipwrecks that he might encounter once he leaves all the comfort and security by the hearth behind. Finally, just as the reader is about to think that the speaker is discouraged from his *wanderlust* by its gloomy prospect, there comes another switch in the last line. The conjunction at the beginning of the line serves, as in Villon's refrain, to suggest a pause and a switch. By adding a comma and have it followed by an apostrophe, Mallarmé further emphasizes the pause, which highlights all the contradictions, the internal struggle, the self-questioning, in the speaker's mind. The temptation of a different life is highlighted in the suggestive expression *le chant des matelots*. Although the poet comes to a sudden ending without telling us about his final decision, his ecstatic response is nevertheless implied in the force of the apostrophe addressed to the speaker himself (*mon coeur*), preceded by the sudden outburst of an emotional exclamation. Like a flash of lightening, the powerful closure illuminates the entire poem.

Let us give another example. Among French poets Rimbaud has been critically acclaimed for his surprise endings. *Le Dormeur du val* (*The One who Sleeps in the Valley*), a poem that he wrote in 1870, is a good illustration of his virtuoso use of such an ending for its psychological effect on the reader:

C'est un trou de verdure où chante un rivière
Accrochant follement aux herbes des haillons
D'argent; où le soleil, de la montagne fière,
Luit: c'est un petit val qui mousse de rayons.

Un soldat jeune, bouche ouverte, tête nue,
Et la nuque baignant dans le frais cresson bleu,
Dort; il est étendu dans l'herbe, sous la nue,
Pâle dans son lit vert où la lumière pleut.

Les pieds dans les glaïeuls, il dort. Souriant comme
Sourirait un enfant malade, il fait un somme:
Nature, berce-le chaudement: il a froid.

Les parfums ne font pas frissonner sa narine;
Il dort dans le soleil, la main sur sa poitrine
Tranquille. Il a deux trous rouges au côté droit.

[It's a hole of greens where a stream sings,
Catching crazily, to the grass, rags
Of silver; where the sun of the proud mountain
Shines: 'tis a little vale foaming with rays of light.

A young soldier, with his mouth open, his head bare,
And his nape bathing in fresh blue cress,
Sleeps; he is spread out in the grass, under the sky,
Pale in his green bed over which the light rains.

He sleeps, with his feet in gladiola. Smiling as
A sick child would be, he takes a nap:
Nature, rock him warmly: he is cold.

The fragrance does not make his nostrils quiver;
He sleeps in the sun, one hand on his chest, that is
Tranquil. He has two red holes in his right side.]

The scene is set in a beautiful and seemingly peaceful valley through which a stream flows and over which the sun shines from above the mountains. The person in the scene is a young soldier stretched out in the green grass, "sleeping." Both the title (*Le Dormeur*) and the text itself, all the way until the ending, make up an elaborate disguise to cover up the hard fact. At a first reading of the poem the reader most likely would not realize the horrible death of the soldier until the last line, and only after the irregular *césure*, set after the word *Tranquille*, used as a *rejet*, and underscored by the use of a period. (Incidentally the *césure* is set after the second syllable rather than the sixth as required by the form of the alexandrine line.) The word *Tranquille* forms a sharp contrast with the subsequent sentence that reveals the truth (the soldier has been shot dead), and thus creates a strong tension. Now, when we read the poem for the second time, our realization of what has really happened from the ending sheds light upon the sinister anticipating significance of some of the words along the way, such as the word *Pâle* in line 8, and the sentence *il a froid* in line 11. The word *trou* (of the land) in the first line corresponds to the *trous* (in the right side of the soldier's body) in the last line. The ending, with its seemingly cool and objective revelation of the cruel truth, makes some of the previous description (*Souriant comme / Sourirait un enfant malade*) stand out strikingly in their presentation of the horror of a tragic death.

Western poetry has countless examples of what may be called *epiphany closure*. The importance of the final couplet in William Shakespeare's sonnets, for instance, has been too widely acknowledged to need any further discussion within the scope of this study. Such endings sometimes provide the sudden realization of truth, as, for instance, in Philip Sidney's famous first poem of his sonnet sequence, *Astrophil and Stella*. After devoting all previous lines to telling how the poet wrestles with the difficulties of writing while suffering from the frustration in an unsuccessful courtship, the poet makes a sudden twist in the closing line:

"Foole," said my Muse to me, "looke in thy heart and write."

Michael Drayton's sixty-first sonnet in his sequence *Idea* is also a good example of how a surprise ending would play the *dominant* function of turning all previous lines upside down and thus determine the very nature of the whole poem. The poem is about a lovers' quarrel, about the misery of separation and the joy of reunion. In the octave the speaker assumes an almost indifferent language in talking about their imminent break:

Since there's no helpe, Come let us kisse and part;
Nay, I have done: You get no more of Me,
And I am glad, yea glad with all my heart
That thus so cleanly, my Selfe can free,
Shake hands forever, Cancell all our Vowes,
And when we meet at any time againe,
Be it not seene in either of our Browes
That We one jot of former Love retaine;...

Then, at the beginning of the sestet, there seems to be a switch in tone, as the speaker begins to talk about his suffering in sharp contrast to the insouciant attitude as shown in previous lines:

> Now at the last gaspe of Loves latest Breath,
> When, his Pulse failing, Passion speechlesse lies,
> When Faith is kneeling by his bed of Death,
> And Innocence is closing up his Eyes,
> Now, if thou would'st, when all have given him over,
> From Death to Life, thou might'st him yet recover.

At the ending, by using the strongly contrasting pair of antonyms, *life* and *death*, as well as by the heart-rending appeal which forms a contrast with the apparently nonchalant tone in the beginning, the whole poem is placed under a new light: all the passion, hope and desire of the relation reveal themselves from out of the disguise of indifference. Just as in the examples of beginnings discussed above, the *dominance* of such a closure is equally obvious.

Poetic Closure: Ending as New Opening

On more careful investigation into the issue of poetic closure, we find that a marked difference seems to exist between Chinese and Western poetry and poetics. Talking in general terms can hardly avoid generalizations; but talking about such two great but widely different traditions can hardly avoid talking in general terms. Bearing in mind that there are always exceptions to any generalization, I shall venture to make the observation here that while Western poetry stresses *consummation* in a poetic text, Chinese poetry tries to point to *what is beyond the text itself*. Thus Western poets would in general aim at *completion* in the ending, whereas Chinese poets would try to leave something *incomplete*. What Western poets have aimed to have, and what Western readers in general have expected, at the ending of the poetic text, to use Barbara Herrnstein Smith's term, is a kind of *closure* indeed. The Chinese poets, on the other hand, have considered it a superb skill to introduce at the ending a kind of new *opening*. Under such a consideration, although the Latin-origin term *closure* (from *clausura*, a principal form of the verb *claudere*, "to shut or close") will still be adopted in this study, it should be noticed here that the word is used throughout the book with some restrictions. It is defined, within the scope of this study, not in its etymological meaning with a sense of finality and completion, but as a synonym to the word *ending* that originated from Old English, which simply suggests an act of putting an end to the text.[18]

In Chinese poetry there is a type of poetic closure which takes the form of presenting an apparently noncommittal, objective image rather than a subjective statement of thought. The term *image* here is different from what we actually see with our eyes, as a picture or a visual scene. It is, as defined in *The Oxford English Dictionary*, "a mental representation of something (esp. a visible object), not by direct perception, but by memory or imagination." A *poetic image*, then, is a mental picture or description created by the poet in his text, that acts on the reader's mind via linguistic means (often working as simile or metaphor); it is something that may, as Roland Barthes has observed, contain messages.[19] It is something that the reader could conceive, imagine, and interpret through what Wordsworth has called "the inward eye." This study attempts to look into larger issues of comparative poetics through a small window, that of what I propose to call *image closure* or *scenic closure*, one that plays a dominant function in the text in presenting a poetic image.

This book starts with an examination of some exemplary texts, employing such image closure, by Tu Fu, generally acknowledged to be China's greatest poet and indisputably one of its most representative poets. Then, through a diachronic survey of poetic closure in the Chinese tradition, we shall look into the development of such image endings in Chinese poetry, as well as the aesthetic values which have supported and sustained it. When it reached its full form in the High T'ang or "the Golden Age of Chinese Poetry," as illustrated by Tu Fu's texts, the concluding image's effect was closely related to the aesthetic binary opposition of *ching* (scene) and *ch'ing* (emotion). Through an examination of the critical context, I seek to demonstrate how the scenic closure was understood, both by poets and by critics, as a deliberate effort, a desirable technique, to expand and extend what may well be called, in Wolfgang Iser's terminology, the "phenomenological dimensions" of the poetic text.[20]

A number of pre-modern Western poems with similar or approximate endings will then be closely read in this perspective. Some of the questions to be raised and discussed are: Was the scenic closure frequently used in Western poetry before it received any influence from the Orient? Were such endings ever singled out for critical attention? If hardly or never, why? An exploration into these problems, to be followed by a survey of the early reception of Chinese poetry in the West, will help to illuminate some of the basic differences between Chinese and Western poetry.

Though primarily an investigation of poetic structure, this book unfolds itself on the basis of the close reading of a number of poems from both East and West, of various periods and types. A primary aim of the book, as hopefully will be illustrated in the course of such close reading, is to combine traditional Chinese criticism with relevant Western reading skills and critical stances. Literary criticism, however, is not supposed to be an end in itself. The only way to justify its relevance is to bring about what Roland Barthes called the *jouissance* that comes from the reading and appreciation of literature itself.[21] The ultimate goal of a literary critic, in the pure sense of the word, is to reveal, and to enjoy, as and for what Virginia Woolf has called a "Common Reader," all the art and beauty in literature: what makes a literary text *artistic* and *beautiful*. Furthermore, it would be a great satisfaction to such a critic if he can do something to further enrich literature itself, either through making his own writing a genuine part of it, or through providing insight and inspiration for abler writers in their literary practice. The ultimate purpose of a comparative study of literature of East versus West is a comprehensive theory based upon a mutual knowledge of independently evolved traditions, which will in turn, hopefully, help to provide a seedbed for new literary devices, forms, and structures as yet unknown to those traditions.

Notes

1. See Ladislav Matejka and Krystyna Pomorska eds. *Readings in Russian Poetics: Formalist and Structuralist Views* (Ann Arbor: University of Michigan Press, 1978), pp. 16, 20, 161, 221, 226.

2. Cited with omissions indicated by ellipses from *Journals of Dorothy Wordsworth: The Alfoxden Journal, 1798* [and] *The Grasmere Journals, 1800–1803, with an Appendix of Wordsworth's Shorter Poems referred to in the Journals*, ed. with an Introduction by Helen Darbishire (London: Oxford University Press, 1963), pp. 142–43. (*The Grasmere Journal 1800–1803*: April 1802, Thursday 15th.) The italics are mine.

3. Roman Jacobson, "The Dominant," in Matejka and Pomorska, pp. 82–90.

4. This is in K'ung Ying-ta's note to a quotation of two lines from the *Shih ching*,

in his scholiasm of the *Chung-yung* (*Centrality and Commonality*). See his *Li-chi chu-shu, Ssu-pu pei-yao* Edition, (Shanghai: Chung-hua shu-chü, 14 Vols., 1933), *chüan* 53, p. 10b. What K'ung meant by the term was to take a quotation out of its context, adopt only its meaning on the surface, and thus deviate from the original.

5. Lu Chi, *Wen fu*, in Kuo Shao-yü and Wang Wen-sheng eds. *Chung-kuo li-tai wen-lun hsüan* (Shanghai: Ku-chi, 4 Vols., 1979), I, pp. 170–89. See also Ch'ien Chung-shu's discussion of the term *ching-ch'e* in his *Kuan chui p'ien* (Peking: Chung-hua, 4 Vols., 1979), III, pp. 1196–98. The *Wen fu* has been rendered into several English translations. See the most recent one, with extensive critical notes, by Stephen Owen in his *Readings in Chinese Literary Thought* (Cambridge, Massachusetts: Harvard University Press, 1992), pp. 73–181; for the *Wen fu* quotation discussed here see pp. 146–48; for a bibliography of related Western readings see p. 649.

6. Chou Chen-fu ed. *Wen-hsin tiao-lung chu-shih* (Peking: Jen-min wen-hsüeh ch'u-pan-she, 1981), pp. 462–68. The work has got a complete English translation, Vincent Y.C. Shih, *The Literary Mind and the Carving of Dragons* (New York: Columbia University Press, 1959). For a selected translation with critical notes see Owen, *Readings*, pp. 183-298; for the two chapters discussed here see pp. 251–55, 267–72.

7. Fang Hsüan-ling et al. *Chin shu*, *chüan* 92, (Peking: Chung-hua shu-chü, 12 Vols., 1974), VIII, pp. 2404–06.

8. In Wang Ta-p'eng et al. eds. *Chung-kuo li-tai shih-hua hsüan* (Ch'angsha: Yüeh-lu shu-she, 2 Vols., 1985), I, pp. 70–71.

9. Kuo and Wang, II, pp. 423–29. See Owen's translation and critical notes in his *Readings*, pp. 391–420; for this quotation see pp. 399–401.

10. Hu Shih, *Pai-hua wen-hsüeh shih* (Ch'angsha: Shang-wu yin-shu-kuan, Fourth Edition, 1938), pp. 171–80. See also Hu Shih, "The Indianization of China: A Case Study in Cultural Borrowing," in *Independence, Convergence, and Borrowing in Institutions, Thought, and Art, Harvard Tercentenary Publications* (Cambridge, Massachusetts: Harvard University Press, 1937), pp. 219–47.

11. George Gordon Byron, *Don Juan*, IV, i. See *Poetical Works* (London: Oxford University Press, 1904), p. 699.

12. From stanza 14 of Longfellow's *Elegiac Verse*.

13. See Pierre Legouis, "The Dramatic Elements in Donne's Poetry," in Helen Gardner ed. *John Donne: A Collection of Critical Views* (Englewood Cliffs, N.J.: Prentice-Hall, 1962), pp. 36–51.

14. See Shen Te-ch'ien, *Shuo-shih ts'ui-yü ch'üan-p'ing*, *chüan* 1, ed. with Commentary by Su Wen-ch'o (Hong Kong: Chih-hao shu-chü, 1978), p. 130.

15. From Lu Ch'in-li ed. *Hsien-Ch'in Han Wei Chin Nan-Pei ch'ao shih* (Peking: Chung-hua shu-chü, 3 Vols., 1983), I, p. 451.

16. All English translations of poems and texts in other languages in the book are my own unless otherwise specified.

17. This is the opening lines of Li Po's *Song of Lu-shan to be Mailed to Lu Hsü-chou the Imperial Attendant* (*Lu-shan yao tseng Lu shih-yü Hsü-chou*), from the *Ch'üan T'ang shih*, *chüan* 173 (Shanghai: Chung-hua shu-chü, 25 Vols., 1985), V, p. 1773.

18. Barbara Herrnstein Smith, *Poetic Closure: A Study of How Poems End* (Chicago: University of Chicago Press, 1968), viii. See also David Hult, "Editor's Preface" in *Concepts of Closure* (New Haven, Connecticut: Yale University Press, 1984), *Yale*

French Studies 67, iii–vi. Hult discussed the difference between the two words *closure* and *end*, and took the latter as a nominal form in contrast to the verbal form of the former. However, here I am referring to the gerundial form *ending* so that an act (that of putting an end to the text) is also implied.

19. Roland Barthes, "Rhetoric of the Image," *Image-Music-Text*, essays selected and translated by Stephen Heath (New York: Hill and Wang, 1977), pp. 32–51.

20. Wolfgang Iser, "The Reading Process: A Phenomenological Approach," in Jane P. Tompkins ed., *Reader-Response Criticism: From Structuralism to Post-Structuralism* (Baltimore: Johns Hopkins University Press, 1980), pp. 50–69.

21. See Barthes, *Le plaisir du texte* (Paris: Seuil, 1973).

2

Scenic Closure in Tu Fu's Poetry

IN the changing canons of poetry and poetics, Tu Fu has always occupied a central position among classical Chinese poets. Historically he stood at a middle point of the development of Chinese poetry. By his both innovative and synthetic practice he was indisputably the most important figure in the High T'ang, traditionally considered as the Golden Age of Chinese poetry.

More frequently than any of his contemporaries, Tu Fu had an inclination for the *meta-poetic*. He frequently discussed poets, poetry, and the problems of poetic composition in his own poems. On two such occasions the issue of poetic closure was raised. In his sequence *in memorium* entitled *Eight Laments* (*Pa ai shih*) there was one in memory of Chang Chiu-ling, an elder poet and statesman. Tu Fu, who often spoke warmly of the works of his peers, paid a compliment to the ending of Chang's poems:

> A poem is done, yet leaving further space,
> The text ends where words are lucid and terse. (VII, 2355)[1]

In a poem addressed to his friends and Kao Shih and Ts'en Shen, both important poets of the age, Tu Fu also touched on the subject:

> At peace, the mind flies, soaring high;
> The text, at its end, joins the vast. (2427)

What kind of *further space* is left after the poem is finished? What is meant by the *vast* that the text joins at the end? Presumably it refers, not to the literal blank subsequent to the end of every literary text, but to an extended semantic dimension, one that allows more room for the author's thought beyond what is apparent in the text, to be further explored, and hopefully to be concretized, by the reader. It is an invisible continuation of the text itself that is nevertheless established by something in the visible part of the text, particularly by something at the end. The concept of such a *further space* or *vast* seems to correspond to Chung Hung's definition of the *hsing* (affective / associational image), the critical term that developed from the scholia of the *Shih-ching* (*The Book of Songs*): "The writing stops, but the meaning goes on." (*wen yi chin erh yi yu yü*).[2] While Chung Hung was talking about a kind of literary mode in general sense, Tu Fu, in the context of these two poems, was obviously making specific comments on poetic closure.

More evidently than in Chang Chiu-ling's existent poems, Tu Fu's own poetry, as was pointed out by one of Tu Fu's commentators, often exemplified what he described in those meta-poetic remarks above.[3] The following occasional poem illustrates Tu Fu's own practice of creating such *further space* or *vast*:

Song of Fowls-Trussing (*Fu chi hsing*)

My servant boy was trussing up fowls to sell them in the market;
Ruffled with the binding, the fowls clucked in struggle.
My family loathed the fowls for they would eat the insects—the ants,
Not knowing that, once sold, they would in turn be boiled and eaten.
Insects, fowls—why should one be dearer to humans than the other?
I shouted to the servant, to have the fowls untied at once.
Fowls, insects—what an endless course of gain and loss!
Gazing at the cold river, I leaned on the hillfort wall. (2235)

Let us start a close reading of the poem from a discussion of its title. In her study of poetic closure, Barbara Herrnstein Smith has suggested that poetic titles frequently serve precisely the purpose of indicating the occasion of the poem, and that they do not describe or define the contents of the poem so much as set it up. Accordingly, she has argued that titles may be regarded as one of the poet's linguistic resources of the poet, or somehow as one of the external clues to the context of a poem, along with dates of composition, epigraph quotations, and perhaps the poet's very name.[4] Most titles do serve the restricted purpose of setting the poem up as Smith has maintained, but even when we restrict our scope of discussion to Western poetry alone, we may find poetic titles which play a more significant structural role. In some of William Carlos Williams's poems (*This Is Just To Say, The Yachts, These,* etc), for example, the title may either be a part of the first line (as its grammatical subject), or sometimes even the first line by itself, thus forming an integral part of the entire poem.

In classical Chinese poetry, what we read as a title today was frequently not given by the poet himself, but rather coined up by the compiler or the publisher, who assigned it for technical reasons. However, since the T'ang dynasty, the title has captured an increasing attention from both the poet and the reader as an important structural part. With the rise and development of the form of the *lü-shih* (regulated verse) a practice of *p'o-t'i* (literally, "disassembling or dissecting the title") was established, which was to have different elements of the title amplified within the poem itself. This practice may have derived from the convention of civil service examinations, during which the candidates were assigned a title by the examiner (occasionally the emperor himself), and were required to compose a poem bearing that title. An important criterion of the poem was how well it adhered to and developed on that title. Thus in traditional Chinese poetry the title became something that the poet had in mind in the process of composition, and that the reader also had in mind in the process of reading and appreciation.

In the case of Tu Fu's poem cited above, the title, which seems to be a relatively simple one, nevertheless calls for a more careful examination. The term *hsing* in the original title (rendered as *Song* in the translation) indicates its sub-generic features. The *hsing* was one of the lyric sub-genres in the *yüeh-fu* ("Music Bureau") tradition of the Han dynasty, established in the Martial Emperor's (*Wu-ti*) reign (141–87 B.C.). It conventionally adopted a number of fixed, usually more formal or serious topics such as *Watering the Horses at the Great Wall Grottoes*, *The Governor of Yen-men*, *Joining the Army*, *The Orphan*, etc.[5] In this poem, however, as in several other *hsing* texts of Tu Fu's, such a commonplace topic as *Fowls-Trussing* was virtually unprecedented for the sub-genre. A tension between generic convention and thematic innovation thus already builds itself up in the title. Why was the poet using a conventional form, usually carrying more serious themes, for such a quotidian trifle? Did he have any important message to give in doing so? If so, what was the message?

If the poem is to be considered in the light of the Formalist concept of *fabula* and *sjuzet*, then the former, the basic material of the occasion of the poem, is apparently an undramatic event in daily life. What concerns us here is the latter, the artistic arrangement that creates the dramatic and lyrical out of the ordinary and prosaic, that transfers the account of a trifle into a lyric *Song*. Tu Fu once claimed that he was "an eccentric by nature who indulged in exquisite lines" (2443), and that towards his later years he began to "pay increasing attention to versifying details" (2586). In the hands of a master like Tu Fu, very little in his later poems is found to be casual.

In a poem such as this one, Tu Fu's art lies in creating an appearance of casualness and ease. The first six lines provide a matter-of-fact description of the occasion. The language of these lines is simple and straight, almost monotonous. The word *chi* (*fowls*) is used five times—once in each of the first five lines. The word *fu* (variously rendered as *trussing up, binding,* and un*tied* in the translation) appears three times, in lines 1, 2, and 6. On the other hand, the respective position of these words varies in each line. Such repetition of diction, as well as the prosaic language in general, is actually a deliberate, skillful way to capture the natural rhythm and retrieve the plain tone of talking about an apparently trivial subject.

Line 7 is an important transitional line. By inserting the phrase *gain and loss* (*te shih*), the poet shifts from the simple, straight account in previous lines to philosophical meditation. There is also a reversal of order of the words *fowls* and *insects* from line 5, which insinuates the balancing and counter-balancing of *gain and loss* in the poet's mind.

The ending, on first reading, seems to be entirely irrelevant. It does not seem to follow the previous lines in a logical order. In presenting an image of himself, leaning against the wall of his residence up the hill and gazing at the cold river, the poet seems to have let his thought go off at a tangent.[6] In what sense is this image related to the occasion? What connections are there between the cold river beneath the poet and the fowls pecking at the insects? The ambiguity of the ending of the poem has puzzled, for example, one of its Western translators, as is shown in the following German translation of the poem:

Die Geschichte von den gebundenen Hühnern

Mein Bursche bindet die Hühner, um sie nach dem Markte zum Verkaufe zu bringen.
Die Hühner sind fest gebunden und kämpfen lärmend mit einander.
Die Leute des Hauses wollen von den Hühnern nichts wissen, weil sie Insekten und Ameisen verspeisen (Lebewesen vernichten).
Sie verstehen nicht, dass die Hühner,—wenn verkauft—doch auch gebraten werden.
Wer von beiden, Insekten oder Hühner, gilt fur den Menschen mehr (warum Mitleid haben mit Insekten und nicht mit Hühnern)?
Ich befehle daher dem Burschen, die Bande den Hühner zu lösen.

Die Frage, ob man den Hühnern oder den Insekten Schutz angedeihen lassen muss, lasst sich niemals entscheiden.
Mein Blick festigt sich auf den kalten Strom, während ich gegen die Wand der Bergklause (des Westturmes) lehne (d.h. ich suche die Frage zu vergessen).[7]

Translation is itself an interpretation. Here the translator, Erwin von Zach, was an industrious Austrian sinologist who made substantial contributions to the field through his meticulous translation of classical Chinese literature. However, by feeling obliged to explain the last line parenthetically ("i.e. I try to forget the question"), he tactlessly "drew a snake and then added feet to it" (*hua she t'ien chu*), as the Chinese idiom goes, at the end of the poem.[8] It is not only a superfluous addition that limited the richness of the text; it is a misreading.

The very act of composing a poem is an act of remembering rather than forgetting. By presenting an image rather than making a statement at the end of the poem, Tu Fu was not trying to "forget the question," as von Zach's parenthetical note suggested, but rather to reflect upon many things beyond the question itself. One statistical study of Tu Fu's poetry indicates that this poem, despite its seemingly ordinary content and its generally prosaic language, has nevertheless been among a choice group of the most anthologized Tu Fu texts, which consists of a tenth of Tu Fu's *oeuvre* of about fourteen hundred.[9] The canonizing of this poem is probably to be credited, to a large extent, to its ambiguous closure, through which the poet's thought, far more complex than the simple occasion itself, finds an elevated expression in the text.

In reading a poem we are constantly playing a mental game of filling in the "spots of indeterminacy" between the lines, to search for things left unsaid from what is being said. It is the unarticulated reply to the question raised in line 5—that humans have no reason to side with either fowls or insects, that leads to the action described in line 6: the poet shouted to the servant to set the fowls free. Yet, by doing so, the poet is contradicting himself: he is now taking side with the fowls, and the release of the fowls means the doom of more insects. At first, the *gain* of the insects (for getting rid of the fowls who would eat them), and the *gain* of humans (for those who may buy the fowls in the market for food, and for the poet and his family who can get some money back from the bargain and also feel at ease about the insects), would have become the *loss* of the fowls. But now, the *gain* of the fowls (in not being sold and consequently not to be boiled and eaten) has turned out to be the *loss* of the insects. In addition, are not the *gain and loss* for human beings very much like those of the fowls and the insects? One's gain may be the loss of another, and a loss for the time being may precede a gain sometime later, and vice versa. This is the lesson from the ancient Chinese fable of the old man on the frontier losing and regaining his horse (*sai weng shih ma*).[10] Isn't all this *an endless course* indeed?

All the complex odds and ends of thinking are left out of the text, which closes in no more than an image of the poet standing there, silent and solitary, in a desolate winter scene on the riverside. Stylistically, the language of the last line has notably turned into the lyrical, forming a sharp contrast with the prosaic tone in the first six lines.

An examination of the biographical, historical, and literary background of the poem may help further reveal its rich texture. *Song of Fowls-Trussing* was generally dated in the winter of 766, four years before the poet's death.[11] Earlier in the autumn, Tu Fu had moved to the mountain city of K'uei-chou. After the death in the preceding year of his patron, Yen Wu the Military Commissioner (regional governor), he had almost given up all hope of ever having the chance to return to the capital and serve in the imperial court. in addition to his disillusion in a political career, the poet was feeling alienated, nostalgic, and restless, and found it ever so difficult to reconcile himself to destiny. During this period, although Tu Fu was constantly questioning the ultimate significance of his status as a poet, he still could not forget his early ambition to serve in the imperial court: "To help elevate the sovereign above Yao and Shun / And once again purify our habits and morale" (2252). Meanwhile, this period also found Tu Fu at the height of his poetic power. Tu Fu was primarily a Confucian who cherished the ideal of staying actively "in the world" (*ju shih*), rather than living passively "out of the world" (*ch'u shih*). To him a secluded life at a remote mountain town, a life in which he had nothing better to do than drawing lessons from daily trifles, was more a suffering than a pleasure.

The poem is rich with literary allusions. The poet's gazing of the cold river at the end was a gesture with both temporal and spatial suggestions. It immediately reminds a Chinese reader the famous remark Confucius made while standing by a river: "The passing [time] is like this [river] indeed, flowing on day and night."[12] The running waters of a river have always made a symbol of the fleeting time and called to attention the brevity of human life span. Placed in the chronological context of Tu Fu's works, the scene of the poet gazing at the river in this poem is reminiscent of the irretrievably lost prime of his life. Admittedly the poet was only fifty-five years old that winter. But, following a norm of Chinese lyric convention, Tu Fu had started lamenting the frustration and suffering of aging as early as in his late thirties. One may also relate the season (presumably winter from the phrase *cold river*) with the approaching dusk of the poet's life. Furthermore, in Tu Fu's late poems, the Yangtze was often seen as a means to carry him away from the restrictive world in Szechuan, down to the lake regions which may then lead him north back to the capital, a means to get "over there" away from *here and now*, as an avenue of escape or return.

The central theme of the poem is choice. As noticed by some critics, the poet's decision to have the fowls untied parallels a story in the *Book of Mencius*. The king of Ch'i (Hsüan-wang) once saw someone leading an ox through the courtyard. On inquiring where the ox was being led to, the king was told that it was to be killed as a sacrifice, with its blood smeared over a newly wrought bronze bell, a common ritual of the time. Then the king said: "Release it. I couldn't bear to see it shivering. It is innocent, and should not be put to death." But was the ritual to be abolished? No, said the king, but replace it with a lamb. Mencius grabbed the occasion to persuade the king into carrying out a moral, virtuous reign. He suggested to the king that the reason why His Majesty substituted the ox with a lamb was not, as understood among his people, due to his stinginess, even though an ox was indeed bigger and more expensive than a lamb. Nor was it really because, as the king himself maintained, that he felt pity for the innocent ox facing an undue death. Wasn't the lamb just as innocent? So why did the king make such a choice? The main reason, argued Mencius, was that the king actually saw the ox shivering but not the lamb, and thereby showed a humane heart in himself, which would serve as a solid basis for a humane reign. Mencius said:

> This is the way a gentleman (*chün-tzu*) treats an animal: When he sees it alive, he cannot bear to see it die; when he hears it cry, he cannot bear to eat its flesh. This is why a gentleman keeps himself far away from the kitchen.[13]

The parallel between the two events is obvious. The reason why the poet took side with the fowls, then, was probably because he heard the fowls "clucking," "ruffled with the binding." The fowls were right there in his sight while the insects were not. Through this allusion, in a parallel to the king's choice between the ox and the lamb allegorized in the Confucian classic, the poet's choice between the fowls and the insects in a commonplace daily scene has thereby assumed a rich, subtle significance, not only for the poet himself, but also, in a larger historical sense, for human beings in general.

The image of the poet standing alone (*tu li*), as presented in the closing line of the poem, is a recurrent one in Tu Fu's poetry. An earlier poem, *Song of Pleasure Park* (*Lo-yu Yüan ko*), recounts the poet's experience of getting drunk at a picnic party held in the famous park in the capital city of Ch'ang-an. In the last couplet of the poem, an apparently joyous mood is suddenly switched to an overflow of sad emotions:

> This body of mine, after I get drunk, has no place to go;
> Standing alone in the vast, I chant poetry to myself. (2261)

The switch of emotions here follows the age-old pattern of "sadness lies where joy comes to extreme" (*le chi sheng pei*) as in, for example, the famous *Song of Autumn Wind* (*Ch'iu-feng tz'u*) attributed to the Martial Emperor of the Han dynasty. Rather than making an account of his sad feelings, the poet closes the poem by an image of himself standing alone, chanting the poem to himself with no one in the audience.

The following poem, entitled *Standing Alone* (*Tu li*), may serve as another inter-textual note for the closure of *Fowls-Trussing*:

> A bird of prey out in the void,
> A pair of white gulls along the river.
> The one, soaring high, is ready to strike,
> The couple move to and fro, fully at ease.
> The grass is mostly wet with dew drops,
> The spider is yet to fetch the trapped in its web.
> Nature's ways are so close to human affairs;
> I stand alone, sad in thoughts of a myriad causes. (2424)

In this poem Tu Fu uses highly allegorical language to weave an underlying message. As traditional interpretation goes, this poem implies how virtuous people are in constant danger of being framed by the evil and sinister. The closure extends the thematic dimension from the particular to the general: the poet, standing alone, is sad in thoughts of *a myriad causes*. Instead of telling us directly what these thoughts are about, he just provides a closing image of himself standing alone in brooding. The clue to decoding of that message probably lies in the penultimate line. What the poet had just witnessed as "Nature's ways" (*t'ien chi*), the troubling scene of a predatory bird about to swoop upon the white gulls, who were unaware of the coming danger, reminded him of all the hidden dangers and risks in human affairs as, for example, in all the schemes and conspiracies of court politics.

By presenting the image of a structured gesture rather than giving an account of his feelings, the closure of *Fowls-Trussing* is a sign of unspoken depth of reflection that draws the reader to similar reflections in the interpretative process. In this way a mere trifle in the poet's ordinary secluded life is turned into a highly intensive lyrical drama. The allusion to the story in *Mencius* in the poem exemplifies the art, in the critical term of the Sung poet Huang T'ing-chien, "to tap iron and transform it into gold" (*tien t'ieh ch'eng chin*).[14]

The brilliance of the closure was widely noticed by later critics. The Sung poet Ch'en Shih-tao remarked that the concluding line of this poem "holds profound and lasting significance in reserve" (*chi t'o shen yüan*). In his comments on this poem Chao Yen-ts'ai, a Sung scholiast of Tu Fu's poetry, even went further to maintain in general terms that "the excellence of a poem lies entirely in the last line (*lo-chü*)."[15] Hung Mai, another Sung scholar, did a witty job by citing Tu Fu's *Song of Fowls-Trussing* side by side with a poem by Li Te-yüan, a Sung poet:

Song of Boats East and West (*Tung hsi ch'uan hsing*)

Boats east, on the wind, hoist the sails high and full,
Go a thousand miles in a wink, light as goose feather.
Boats west, butts of ridicule, plod along in pain,
A hundred punt-poles get broken in their sweating toil.
But next day, when wind and waves change direction,
Boats west will scorn those east in the same way.
East, west, they mock each other in an endless course;
While I follow Nature's way, to hide, or to emerge.[16]

Hung Mai did not elaborate on the relative values of the two poems. The conspicuous difference between the endings of these two poems speaks for itself. Li Te-yüan's poem closes in a way the reader would normally expect to find in an allegorical poem: a philosophical conclusion on the subject matter; little room is left there for the reader's own reflections; but a poem can be much richer in its meaning without such a closure of explicit statement, as is shown in the example of the Tu Fu text.

Song of Fowls-Trussing is not the only Tu Fu poem in which he made use of the scenic closure. The poet frequently resorted to its use for specific poetic effects. At his hands, the use of the scenic closure as a dominant poetic structural part is rich in variations.

Moonlit Night (*Yüeh yeh*) is one of Tu Fu's most celebrated early poems, and probably one of the greatest Chinese poems about family love and the sorrow of separation:

Tonight, over Fu-chou, the moon
In her boudoir she watches all alone.
From afar I miss our little sons and daughters
Who know not yet recalling Ch'ang-an.
Perfumed mist: cloud—tresses—moist,
Serene beams: white jade—arms—cold.
When, leaning by diaphanous curtains, shall stand
We two, with our tear stain dry in moonshine? (2403)

This poem was dated in the year of 756, when the poet was detained by An Lu-shan's rebel troops at Ch'ang-an, separated from his wife and children who were living at Fu-chou county about 175 miles north of the capital.

The poem is about the pain of separation and the tenderness of family love. The former emerges in spatial terms through the use of the two geographic names, Fu-chou and Ch'ang-an, in lines 1 and 4. The distance between the two places is underscored by the first two lines that present an imaginary scene of his wife gazing at the moon, a traditional symbol of union (when it waxes to full) and separation (when it wanes). Tu Fu is a master of using contrast. Here, in a poem in the form of the pentasyllabic *lü-shih*, he combines the device of contrasting images with the use of antithesis, the latter being a formal requirement.

The first or the *head* couplet (*shou-lien*, to use traditional structural terms for *lü-shih*) presents an image of his wife gazing at the moon alone in her boudoir. In the second or the *chin* couplet (*han-lien*) the poet switches from *there* (Fu-chou) to *here* (Ch'ang-an), from his wife to himself, and expresses his tender feelings towards their children who, unlike their mother, are yet too young to recall their father and the days when the whole family lived together in the capital before the rebellion.[17] Though conforming to the *lü-shih* regulations in tonal pattern, this couplet does not adhere to the syntactical demand of antithesis: "little sons and daughters" (*hsiao erh nü*) do not parallel "recalling Ch'ang-an" (*yi Ch'ang-an*). In Tu Fu's time, especially in a poem of such an intimate topic, the poet would not yet feel restrained by prosodic laws, stipulated in the more rigid convention established in later centuries, to restrict the force of his emotions. The language of this couplet is simple and natural, as befitting the emotions conveyed in it.

The third or the *neck* couplet (*ching-lien*) forms a sharp contrast with the previous couplet in its highly elliptical language and exquisite imagery. His wife's image is presented in *synecdoche*: a rhetoric device that leaves blanks for the reader to fill in with imagination. Here she appears only in her cloud-like locks, fragrant in the mist of the night, and her arms like white jade exposed in the moonlight. If one traces what is left unsaid from between the lines, then one may deduce that she may have stayed at the open window of her chamber for a long time—this would account for her hair getting moist and her arms feeling cold, and why would she stay there watching the moon for so long? What remains implicit here is her deep loving affection for the poet, as is his for her.

The last or the *tail* couplet (*wei-lien*) provides a hypothetical anticipation. The imaginary reunion takes shape in a question, which in its uncertainty sets the fact of their present separation in strong relief, like a dark shadow looming in the moonlit scene. The poem also adopts a scenic closure: the image of the couple reunited on another moonlit night in the future, standing by the window curtains which look almost transparent because of the bright moonlight shining through them. Those tears are happy tears, tears that loving spouses would shed at reunion after long separation. The language is highly figurative: the moonlight is attributed the mysterious power to dry up their tears. The word *shuang* ("we two") in the last line, suggestive of the imaginary reunion in an unpredictable future, harks back to its antonym *tu* ("alone") used in the second line. Corresponding to the implication of the length of the wife's stay at the window (long enough to get her hair moist and her arms cold), the closure is highly symbolic, almost surrealistic: they would stand there long enough to let the moonlight dry up their tear stain—a figure rather unusual in Chinese poetic tradition. The theme of the pain of separation and the aspiration for reunion, the hard fact of the former and the dubious nature of the latter, finds its climax in the closing scene, which helps to extend the dimensions of the entire text in both spatial and temporal senses.

The next poem (heptasyllabic *lü-shih*), *At the Lan-t'ien Villa of the Ts'ui's on the Double Ninth Day* (*Chiu-ji Lan-t'ien Ts'ui-shih chuang*), has generally been dated to the period when Tu Fu took up an official position in Hua-chou during 758. It is another example of the poet's virtuoso use of the scenic closure:

> Getting old, sad in autumn, I've tried hard to console myself,
> On an impulse, this day I would fully share your gaiety;
> Ashamed that off my short hair my cap still got blown away,
> Laughing, I asked someone else to get it secured again.
> Blue River faraway down a thousand creeks falls,
> Jade Mount vies in height with the cold Twin Peaks.
> Next year, when we meet here again, who'd be fit enough?
> Drunk, I looked closely at the ailanthus. (2403)

The Double Ninth Festival, on the ninth day of the ninth Chinese lunar month (usually in October of the Roman calendar), is a day on which people by custom ascend to some height (a mountain, a tower, or in modern times, the roof or top level of a highrise building) to view the scenery, to hold a drinking party, to eat crabmeat, and to watch the colorful chrysanthemum flowers with one's family or friends. There was also a convention to wear on that day leaves of the strongly scented ailanthus (*chu-yü*), often placed in small bags, which were superstitiously believed to possess the magic power of expelling the evil force and extending one's life.

The head couplet of the poem presents a sharp contrast between his emotion and the occasion: while the word *pei* ("sad") in the first line refers to the poet's own feelings, due to his aging and the saddening season of the autumn (the season that corresponds to a man's later years), the word *huan* ("gaiety") indicates the convivial mood of the party, of which the poet joins only half-heartedly, as suggested by the phrase "on an impulse."

The chin couplet alludes to the well known historical anecdote of Meng Chia, a handsome man of letters of the Chin dynasty who was also the famous poet T'ao Ch'ien's maternal grandfather. During an outing at a Buddhist temple which also took place on the Double-Ninth Day, Meng Chia won the admiration of his colleagues by his composure and grace when the wind blew off his cap.[18] This is an adroit use of allusion for the occasion not only because it was an anecdote of a similar occasion—the Double Ninth Day, but also because the poet once held the same official position (*ts'an-chün* or "military consultant") as that of Meng Chia. The irony and wry humor of the allusion lies in the contrast therein: while Meng Chia was celebrated for his graceful manner, handsomeness and youth, the poet feels ashamed because of his older age ("short hair" means "not much new hair growing out"), and perhaps also a sense of inferiority, in terms of physical beauty and grace, when compared to his legendary precursor.

The neck couplet turns to a description of the scene at the party. Blue River (*Lan-shui*) and Jade Mount (*Yü-shan*) are both in the neighborhood of the Lan-t'ien Villa. The Twin Peaks are those of the Yün-t'ai Mountains. While it is another example of the skillful way of *p'o-t'i* or "dissecting the title," it also provides a shift of view from the trifle about the blown-off cap—a "close shot" taken at a short distance, to a "long shot" of the distant larger background of the party. The occasion is placed into a grand perspective.

The tail couplet presents a question in the penultimate line, which displays a sense of uncertainty about future. The poet is not sure if he will be healthy enough to attend another such party next year since, as he has stated in the first line, he is "[a]ging and feeling sad in autumn." Then, instead of giving an answer, the poem closes with an image, a *tableau vivant*, of the drunken poet himself, looking closely at the ailanthus. The scene seems irrelevant to the previous question. What is the message underlying this gesture? The ailanthus leaves stand for tradition—something that will be worn by generations to come, something that will outlive the poet himself and come back perennially. Thus the closure harks back to the beginning, a lament for his old age and the brevity of human life. All this is left unsaid, just as the question is left unanswered. The poem has closed, but the lingering image of the aging and drunken poet leaves *further space* for the reader to digest and to meditate upon.

The pentasyllabic "old-style" poem *Beautiful Lady* (*Chia-jen*), dated in the year 759 when the poet lived in Ch'in-chou as a civilian, adopts a narrative structure in the *yüeh-fu* tradition. It tells about a beautiful woman who lives a secluded life in an empty valley, having been deserted by her husband. Within the story of the unhappy woman there appear lines (17–18) which carry allusions to the *Analects* and *Songs of the South* (*Ch'u-tz'u*), and from their not usually being related to a poem about females, remind the reader of the allegorical nature of the poem:

> In the mountains, the water of the fountain remains clear,
> Out of the mountains, the water of the fountain turns muddy. (2287)[19]

Next, at the end of the poem, instead of making a comment on her misfortune or giving a final vent of her lament, the poem closes with an image of the lady (ll. 21–24):

> She picked a flower, but not to put in her hair,
> And some juniper berries as well, easily a handful.
> The weather was cold, her jade-green sleeves were thin,
> At sunset she stood, leaning by the slender bamboo.

Here again, as in *Chicken-Trussing*, we have the image of a gesture that is structured in a carefully arranged scene. The term "Beautiful Lady" in the title also alludes to the Confucian gentleman (*chün-tzu*), in the convention of Ch'ü Yüan's *Encountering Sorrow* (*Li-sao*). From the same convention the action of picking flowers and juniper berries carries the symbolic meaning of preserving one's loyalty and personality under adverse situations. But the image in the last two lines, a woman who is not wearing sufficiently warm clothes against the cold weather and standing alone by some slender bamboos (a symbol of nobleness), reminds the reader of the poet's own predicament.[20] As one commentator pointed out, by using a description of the scene (*hsieh-ching*) rather than making a commentary (*yi-lun*), the noble, loyal character of the figure is "hidden beyond words," and the poem thus achieves the "highest poetic quality."[21]

Finally, let us conclude with another fine example of Tu Fu's use of scenic closure. *Night Thoughts on a Voyage* (*Lü-yeh shu-huai*) has been widely acknowledged to be one of the greatest pentasyllabic *lü-shih* texts of all Chinese poetry. As David R. McCraw recently pointed out, this is one of Tu Fu's most-translated and best-analyzed poems that makes one hesitate to add another explication.[22] Still I believe that the poem is so rich in its imagery and layers and layers of significance that it could well use one more close reading.

Slender grasses, soft breeze, by the shore,
Tall mast, lonely boat, at night.
Stars hang over the vast of the level wild,
The moon gushes into the flow of the great river.
Reputation—is it to be won by literary works only?
Civil service: it must have finished in my age and sickness.
Tossed by wind, fluttering, what am I like?
Between heaven and earth, a single gull on the sands. (2489)

The poem starts employing parallelism from the first couplet, which after the middle of the eighth century was usually adopted only for the two "inner couplets" in the middle.[23] The images in this couplet present themselves like a kind of montage. The soft breeze is tangible through a visual scene of the slender grasses along the bank of the river. The tall mast looms out of the darkness, forming a sharp contrast to the slender grasses in size. The grasses are moving (trembling in the breeze), the boat, with its tall mast, stays still (presumably mooring at the bank). However, the grasses along the bank actually represent the static; whereas the boat, even though stopping at the moment, is in fact the mobile, as it will resume its journey next morning. In this couplet, a pair of "binary oppositions" is working: quiescence and motion—the land that stays unchanged through ages, and the boat that is moving, carrying on it the aging poet.[24]

The first couplet presents, as if through a camera eye, a snapshot of close perspective. In the second couplet, the poet makes a sudden movement of that camera, and unfolds in front of the reader's "inward eye" is a "long shot" of grandeur and magnificence. Again there is a contrast between the static (the stars and the plain) and the mobile (river). Temporally there is also a contrast between the permanent and the transient. The flowing great river indicates the fleeting time, as well as the growing age of the poet himself.

Adhering to the convention of title dissection for the *lü-shih* form, after devoting the first two couplets to the first two words in the title, voyage and night (*lü yeh*), the next two couplets deal with the next two words in the title, writing (my) thoughts (*shu huai*). From the symbolic meaning of the flowing river in the fourth line, the poem turns into an examination of the fleeting time and the ultimate meaning of life. Line 5 takes the form of a rhetorical question. To our incorrigible Confucian

Tu Fu his reputation (*ming*) should be acquired by "official merits" (*kung-ming*), not by literary writings. The poet probably recalled Confucius's saying: "One should devote oneself to literary studies only if one has any energy left after one's [social] activities."[25] He never really gave up his high aspirations for civil service. The melancholy question finds a response in the seemingly passive and resigned self-explanation given in the next line (one can almost hear the poet murmuring to himself): that he is supposed to give up his ambition due to his age and sickness. The implied indignation is felt if one recalls that the poet was out of favor at court because of his tactless political involvement.

The last couplet repeats the format of question and answer. Both couplets present a catechism in soliloquy, but each is framed in a different way. One is abstract and discursive, the other vividly pictorial.[26] This time the answer takes the form of a closing simile. Tu Fu always had a particular fascination with the image of the gulls, traditionally used as a symbol of understanding companions for those who are free from worldly concerns.[27] There are many examples of his employment of the image in his works. In this poem, however, he is comparing himself to a lonely gull so small and insignificant against the vast background of "heaven and earth," making it into a straight simile for what the poet feels about himself. There is again a sharp contrast in this last image: that of the vastness, the permanence of heaven and earth, and that of the solitude of the wandering little gull. All his sad thoughts on the intriguing court politics, the war-ridden state, and his personal disillusion and misfortune are crystallized in this closing simile, leaving much room for meditation. The scene has become a signature of reflectivity. Poetic closure as such fully achieves the concept of *further space* and the *vast* beyond the text as the poet himself advocated.

Notes

1. The page numbers here are, as for all T'ang poems cited in this book, from the *Ch'üan T'ang shih* (1706) (Peking: Chung-hua shu-chü, 25 Vols., 1985). The pagination of all further citations from the anthology will be noted parenthetically within the text. For all the Tu Fu poems cited I have also checked many other texts (see *Bibliography*), most notably Kuo Chih-ta ed., *Chiu-chia chi-chu Tu-shih* (1181, *Ssu-k'u ch'üan-shu* ed.,

1788, reprint, Taipei: Ta-t'ung ch'u-pan-she, 1974). I have rendered the Chinese term *hun-mang* as *the vast* (from the English word's archaic and poetic use meaning "an immense space"). Tu Fu used the term on another occasion referring to the Yen-yü Pile, the famous rocky reef projecting in the middle of the Yangtze at the Ch'ü-t'ang Gorge: "To capsize (boats) is the intention of Heaven / Whose divine work *joins the vast*" (VII, p. 2505). Later the Jurchen Chin poet Chou Te-ch'ing borrowed the phrase and used it to describe Tu Fu's poetry: "The divine work of Tzu-mei *joins the vast*." (Yüan Hao-wen ed. *Chung-chou chi*, *chüan* 4.) The term sometimes refers to the primeval state of chaos, as used in the *Chuangtzu*: "Shan-hsing" ("Good Deeds"): "Ancient people live in the chaotic *vast*." See Ch'ien Chung-shu, *T'an-i lu* (Hong Kong: Chung-hua shu-chü, revised edition, 1986), p. 309.

2. Chung Hung, "*Shih p'in* hsü," from Kuo and Wang, I, pp. 308–23. For a short list of English translation and criticism of the work see Owen, *Readings*, p. 650.

3. This is a comment made by Shao Tzu-hsiang, cited in Yang Lun ed. *Tu-shih ching-ch'üan* (Shanghai: Ku-chi ch'u-pan-she, 2 Vols., 1962), p. 271.

4. Smith, p. 18.

5. For an introduction of the *yüeh-fu* tradition see Burton Watson, *Chinese Lyricism: Shih Poetry from the Second to the Twelfth Century, with Translations* (New York: Columbia University Press, 1971), pp. 52–67. For a more recent study of the convention see Joseph R. Allen, *In the Voice of Others: Chinese Music Bureau Poetry* (Ann Arbor: Center for Chinese Studies, University of Michigan, 1992).

6. The "hillfort" in line 8 was the official residence assigned to Tu Fu at the city of K'uei-chou, better known in Tu Fu's poetry as the "Western Tower" (*Hsi ko*).

7. *Tu Fu's Gedichte*, translated by Erwin von Zach, ed. and with an Introduction by James Robert Hightower, *Harvard-Yenching Institute Studies VIII* (Cambridge, Massachusetts: Harvard University Press, 1952), pp. 578–79.

8. The idiom has its origin in an ancient Chinese fable from the *Chan kuo ts'e* (*Records of the Warring States*, *Ch'i ts'e*, 2), which means to ruin the effects by adding something superfluous. See *Ch'eng-yü tz'u-tien*, ed. by the Education Bureau of Ch'ang-chou (Nanking: Chiang-su jen-min ch'u-pan-she, 1981), p. 319. An English phrase approximate in meaning is *to gild the lily*.

9. Ling Tzu-lou, *T'ang-shih hsüan-pen Tu Fu shih ts'ai-hsüan* (Hong Kong: Chu Hai College, 1970). *Song of Fowls-trussing* is listed therein as among a group of 127 Tu Fu poems that have been included in more than six different anthologies.

10. This is from the chapter of "Jen chien hsün" of the *Huainantzu*. See *Ch'eng-yü tz'u-tien*, p. 632.

11. See Liu Meng-k'ang, *Tu Fu nien-p'u* (Hong Kong: Hua-hsia ch'u-pan-she, 1967), p. 107b.

12. This is from the *Lun-yü* (*The Analects*), (IX, "Tzu Han" 16). See Chu Hsi ed. *Ssu-shu chi-chu* (Shanghai: Shih-chieh shu-chü, 1937), p. 59.

13. This is a comment made by Shih Yin in *Chiu-chia chi-chu Tu-shih*, II, 842. The famous early Ch'ing critic Chin Sheng-t'an also elaborated on this. See his *Tu-shih chieh*, ed. by Chung Lai-yin (Shanghai: Ku-chi ch'u-pan-she, 1984), p. 209. For the citation from *The Book of Mencius* (I, "Liang Hui-wang, First Part," 7) see *Ssu-shu chi-chu*, *Mencius*, pp. 9–10.

14. See Huang T'ing-chien's "A Letter in Reply to Hung Chü-fu" (*Ta Hung Chü-fu*

shu), cited in Kuo and Wang, II, pp. 316–20. For a recent discussion of the term see David Palumbo-Liu, *The Poetics of Appropriation: The Literary Theory and Practice of Huang Tingjian* (Stanford: Stanford University Press, 1993), especially pp. 66–67.

15. Both cited in Yang Lun, p. 735.

16. Hung Mai, *Jung-tsai san pi, chüan* 5, from Hua Wen-hsüan ed. *Ku-tien wen-hsüeh yen-chiu hui-pien: Tu Fu chüan* (Peking: Chung-hua shu-chü, 1964), p. 507.

17. Chao Yen-ts'ai observed that the line also carries an allusion to the anecdote from the *Shih-shuo hsin-yü* (*A New Account of "Tales of the World"*). Emperor Chin Yüan-ti, who was driven south by northern invaders and established the Eastern Chin regime in southern China, one day received an envoy from Ch'ang-an, the former Chin capital then occupied by a northern regime. The emperor asked his young son (who was to succeed him as the next emperor, Chin Ming-ti) which was farther away, the sun or Ch'ang-an. "Ch'ang-an is closer," said the boy, "I've never heard of anyone coming from the sun." The next day, when asked the same question at an imperial banquet, the boy gave a different reply. "The sun is closer," he said, "When I raise my head I see the sun, but I cannot see Ch'ang-an." This latter response drove the Emperor and his ministers to tears. See *Chiu-chia chi-chu Tu-shih*, III, p. 1327. The allusion is an appropriate one in Tu Fu's poem because at that time the capital city of Ch'ang-an was also in the hands of northern rebels under An Lu-shan. For the anecdote itself see Hsü Cheng-e ed., *Shih-shuo hsin-yü chiao-chien* (Peking: Chung-hua shu-chü, 2 vols., 1984), (XII, 3), p. 323.

18. *Shih-shuo hsin-yü chiao-chien*, (VII, 16), p. 220.

19. This poem is only partially cited here. It has had many English renditions. For a recent translation of the complete text see David R. McCraw, *Du Fu's Laments from the South* (Honolulu: University of Hawaii Press, 1992), pp. 17–18.

20. For the rich connotations of the four symbolic plants in Chinese culture—the plum, the orchid, the bamboo, and the chrysanthemum, see Huang Yung-wu, "Four Symbolic Plants in Chinese Poetry," translated by Wong Lai-leung, in *Renditions: A Chinese-English Translation Magazine* (Hong Kong: The Chinese University Press), No. 9 (Spring 1978): pp. 71–80.

21. A comment made by Shen Chüeh-shih cited in Yang Lun, p. 230.

22. McCraw, pp. 63–65.

23. For a learned discussion of parallel patterns in lines and couplets of Chinese regulated verse see Yu-kung Kao, "The Aesthetics of Regulated Verse", in Shuen-fu Lin and Stephen Owen ed., *The Vitality of the Lyric Voice:* Shih *Poetry from the Late Han to the T'ang* (Princeton: Princeton University Press, 1986), pp. 332–85, esp. pp. 356–61.

24. For the concept of "binary oppositions" see Jonathan Culler, *Structuralist Poetics: Structuralism, Linguistics, and the Study of Literature* (Ithaca: Cornell University Press, 1975), esp. pp. 14–16, 91–94, 126–27.

25. From the *Analects*, (I, "Hsüeh-erh," 6). *Ssu-shu chi-chu*, p. 3.

26. I owe this idea to Professor Irving Y. Lo, who also alerted me to a close parallel in presenting two sets of questions in the closure of Keats's *Ode to a Nightingale*.

27. The allusion originated from a story in the classic *Liehtzu* (the *Huang-ti* chapter). Someone who lived by the sea idled away his time every day at the beach and kept company with hundreds of gulls there. His father heard about it and asked him to bring some home. The next day, when he went to the beach, the gulls were all flying in the sky and would not come down again.

3

The Book of Songs: Ending in the Beginning

IT has been noticed that Chinese culture has a strong sense of, almost an obsession with, history and the past. Chinese poetry is certainly a strong testimony to such an obsession. It is so strongly history and tradition oriented, to the extent that it may almost be said that no Chinese poem, since the beginning of self-conscious poetic composition, can claim to have existed entirely on its own.

This certainly does not mean that a Chinese poem does not constitute an entity in its own right. It does, but this entity is always related to other texts, either previous or contemporary. A poetic text, unlike a sentient being in Buddhist terms, can never hope to be entirely free from the historical-temporal cycle. Even when a Chinese poem is not a direct response to, or an acceptance of, a challenge posed by previous texts, it nevertheless shares some common ground with the vast body of literary creation before it. It is against this common ground that one must evaluate the accomplishment of a poet and his work.

In the case of Tu Fu, "divinity" (*shen*) was a term he repeatedly used in his meta-poetic comments. In his poetry he frequently referred to the working of this "divinity" behind the poet, but he hardly ever defined the term in an unequivocal way. Only on one occasion, however, did he make a remark on where that "divinity" might come from: "Having read through a myriad volumes / I feel my brush moves as if with *divinity*."[1] "Divinity," then, in Tu Fu's words, arises as a result of extensive reading of the works of masters past and present, especially works of the classical age.

Tu Fu's famous poetic sequence, *Six Quatrains Written To Amuse Myself* (*Hsi wei liu chüeh-chü*) is a much-discussed set of heptasyllabic quatrains devoted to terse, largely figurative meta-poetic commentaries on poets and poetry. In the last quatrain of the sequence, the poet seemed to be making a strong statement of what poetry should be like:

Distinguish and delete sham forms and befriend *Feng* and *Ya*,
To learn from many teachers is the teaching meant for you. (2453)

What Tu Fu argued here was that one should not embrace literary heritage without making judgments, but rather should use one's own discretion to distinguish between what is real and true, such as those poems found in the classic anthology, and what he called *sham forms*, epigonic, untruthful writings. One should also break the narrow bounds of one school, and free oneself from the conventions of one master. In other words, one should read widely and learn everything that might be of use. Notably, Tu Fu mentioned in particular the two sections of lyric songs and festal odes (*Feng* and *Ya*) of the *Shih-ching* (*Book of Songs*) as his models.

On another occasion, Tu Fu instructed his son Tsung-wu on the importance of studying *Selections of Refined Literature* (*Wen-hsüan*), the anthology of Chinese literature compiled in early 6th century that contains literary works of different genres and sub-genres from the pre-Ch'in ages (i.e., before 221–207 B.C.) all the way to the Liang Dynasty (502–557). He told his son to "get conversant with the patterns (*li*) of the *Wen-hsüan*" (2535). Indeed, later critics have often identified such a conversance with the classic in Tu Fu's own poetry, and have agreed that it excels in its creative and original use of the entirety of literary heritage in his age. The Sung poet Huang T'ing-chien even maintained that in Tu Fu's poetry (and in Han Yü's prose) every word had a textual antecedent.[2]

A fuller appreciation of Tu Fu's poetic closure, as well as that of his poetic achievement in general, is not to be attained in the context of Tu Fu's *oeuvre* alone. It entails an examination of poetic structure, of the ways poems end, and to a lesser extent, the ways poems begin, in earlier Chinese poetry.

In every culture the masterpieces of early ancestors set the pattern for later development. The ancient Chinese anthology *Shih-ching*, a collection of three hundred and five lyric songs, festal odes, and ritual hymns, generally acknowledged to have been compiled around 600 B.C., is certainly of no less imposing influence to Chinese literature of later periods than are the Homeric epics to European literature, or *Mahabharata* and *Ramayana* to Indian culture. Unlike those great epic poems which describe the past, a large part of the Chinese classic consists of *shih*, i.e., short, casual lyric songs which primarily sing about the present, the joys and sorrows of everyday life. Although its basic stanzaic and repetitive structure was supplanted by other structures later, *Shih-ching* had its undeniable imprint on the development of Chinese poetry. This was partially because, as one of the Confucian scriptures (*ju-ching*) canonized in the Han dynasty, the anthology became a basic part of the curriculum of Chinese education. Hence the anthology has always been seen by later poets as the origin of and continuing source for the tradition.

To a certain extent, however, one may argue that what set the pattern for later poets was less in the *Shih-ching* texts themselves than in what was said about them through the ages. One of those most often discussed issues was that of the triad of modes, *fu*, *pi*, and *hsing*—terms given to rhetorical devices used in the *Shih-ching* texts. An understanding of the triad, especially of *hsing*, the last and most-discussed of the three, is essential to our discussion of scenic closure.[3]

This triad of terms appeared as early as in the *Great Preface* (*Ta-hsü*), an essay of dubious authorship and dating, but generally considered to be a kind of summary of pre-Ch'in Confucian poetics. It was a preface to *Mao's Scholia* of the *Shih-ching*, so called because they were attributed to Mao Heng and Mao Ch'ang, two early Han scholars with expertise on the anthology. These terms are listed in the essay as among the "Six Principles" (*liu-yi*), along with the *feng*, the *ya*, and the *sung*, terms which are also the names of the three sections of the *Shih-ching*, which may be rendered into English as the *airs*, the *odes*, and the *hymns*.[4]

The order of the listing of these six terms corresponds to a record contained in the *Book of Chou Officialdom* (*Chou-li*), a work probably completed in 3rd century B.C., during the late stage of the Warring States period. This record tells us about the curriculum of the Music Master (*ta-shih*), a member of the Ministry of Rites who took part in musical education at the Chou court and directed the musical aspects of various state ceremonies. It says that he taught "the six (kinds of) poetry (*liu shih*), namely, *feng, fu, pi, hsing, ya, sung*."[5] These early sources never bothered to provide any definition for these terms, with the consequence that they became the object of an ever-going controversy. The fact that *hsing* is the only "Principle" exemplified and illustrated in *Mao's Scholia*, in the brief commentaries on separate *Shih-ching* texts known as the Small Prefaces (*Hsiao-hsü*), further added to the confusion.

K'ung Ying-ta, the T'ang scholar who synthesized the exegetical tradition of *Mao's Scholia* to the *Shih-ching*, made a distinction between the two triads in explaining *feng, ya*, and *sung* as the different "forms" (*t'i*) of the texts, and *fu, pi,* and *hsing* as the different "terms" (*tz'u*) of the pattern (*wen*) of the texts. He remarked:

> *Fu, pi,* and *hsing* are what the *Shih(-ching)* makes use of, while *feng, ya,* and *sung* are what the *Shih* takes its shape in. It is through the first three that the latter three are formed, therefore they are generally referred to as the Principles.[6]

Chu Hsi, the great neo-Confucian thinker of the Sung dynasty whose work on the *Shih-ching* was a milestone in breaking new ground in the interpretation of the texts, basically followed K'ung Ying-ta's explanation of these terms, and referred to *feng, ya,* and *sung* as the "three warps" (*san-ching*), and *fu, pi,* and *hsing* as the "three woofs" (*san-wei*), the former being the "bones" or (*ku-tzu*) or substantial material of the *Shih-ching* and the latter, something that threads through it.[7] With the exception of only a few dissenting voices, it has been generally acknowledged thenceforth that *feng, ya,* and *sung* are generic names, and *fu, pi,* and *hsing* are terms referring to the mode of presentation.[8]

Early efforts to explain this latter triad, which concerns our discussion of poetic closure, were made by two *Shih-ching* scholiasts of the Han dynasty, Cheng Chung and Cheng Hsüan. Fragments of the former's exegesis were frequently cited by K'ung Ying-ta, and the latter was known for his commentary on *Mao's Scholia*, the so-called *Cheng's Commentary* (*Cheng chien*). Cheng Hsüan defined *fu* as "direct statement of the event" (*chih ch'en ch'i shih*). According to Cheng Chung, *pi* is "to compare events to objects" (*pi fang yü wu*), and so "all those using the term *ju* (*as* or *like*) are in the *pi* mode." Cheng Chung explained *hsing* and the order of the triad in some details:

> *Hsing* is to present events through [the description of] objects (*t'o shih yü wu*), therefore *hsing* is to bring up (*ch'i*), to use tropes and analogies so as to bring up and express what is in one's mind. In the *Shih* texts, wherein plants, birds, and beasts are used to express one's thoughts are all *hsing*. The reason why *fu, pi,* and *hsing* are placed in such an order is as follows. Direct statement is the normal (*cheng*) way to talk about an event, thus *fu* prevails in the *Shih* and accordingly comes before *pi* and *hsing*. Although both *pi* and *hsing* use external objects as pretexts, *pi* is explicit and *hsing* is implicit, and so *pi* comes before *hsing*. That *Mao's Scholia* has made specific comments on *hsing* only is because its reasoning (*li*) is implicit.[9]

This explanation is not without its problems; one of which is that in the *Shih-ching*, not all those places where "plants, birds, and beasts are used" are necessarily in the mode of *hsing*. They can just as well be the use of *fu* or *pi*, even as understood in Cheng Chung's own definition of these terms. Nevertheless it provided a point of departure for some of the early literary critics during the Six Dynasties period, who made a few revisions of Cheng Chung's explanation. Chih Yü, in his *Wen-chang liu-pieh-lun* (*On the Development and Classification of Literature*), an early commentary on Chinese literary genres, described *hsing* simply as "words that carry emotions" (*yu kan chih tz'u*).[10] This corresponds to Cheng Chung's earlier interpretation of *hsing* as *ch'i* ("bring up"), to bring up or to stir something in one's mind. Confucius, in discussing the purposes of studying the *Shih-ching*, remarked that reading the anthology can "stir up emotions" (*Shih k'o yi hsing*).[11] This, along with a few similar remarks found in other writings of the age, formed the basis of Confucian pedagogy of the *Shih-ching* in the late Warring States period, when the concept of the "Six Principles" was formed. Since its first appearance in *Mao's Scholia*, however, the term *hsing* had been understood as a mode of expression based on reference to external objects (*wai-wu*). Therefore Chih Yü's remark seemed to be a continuation of the early Confucian convention that confirmed the close interrelation of emotions and objects in literature.

In his ambitious *magnum opus*, the *Wen-hsin tiao-lung*, Liu Hsieh devoted one of its fifty chapters to an exclusive discussion of *pi* and *hsing*. To Liu Hsieh, *pi* is explicit and based on "contiguity" (*fu*), i.e., using analogies in terms of sound, appearance, mind, and occasions. The more "accurate and exact" (*ch'ieh chih*) the analogy is, the better. *Hsing*, on the other hand, is implicit, a mode in which the use of tropes (*t'o yü*) should be tactfully indirect. As an illustration of this, Liu Hsieh cited and observed on the tropes used in the commentaries, known as "Appended Words" (*Hsi-tz'u*), on the ancient classic *The Book of Changes* (*I-ching*): "Although the objects cited in their names are small, the significance from their analogy is great." According to Liu Hsieh, the two modes, originally used in the *Shih-ching*, were both in use until the time of *Songs of the South* (*Ch'u-tz'u*), towards the end of the Warring States period (third century B.C.). It was during the Han Dynasty, when the more profound and soul-stirring style characteristic of the *Shih-ching* texts gave up its dominant place to the overt expository style of the rhyme-prose composition (*fu*), which began to flourish as a literary genre, that the principle of *hsing* disappeared.[12] However, Liu Hsieh focused his discussion on *pi* and provided many illustrations of the term, but failed to throw much light on the definition of *hsing*, which remained vague.

As mentioned in the previous chapter, the most remarkable explanation of *hsing* from the period was given by Chung Hung who, in the preface to his *Categories of Poets* (*Shih-p'in*), added a fine touch to the definition of the term by describing it as a mode by the use of which "the writing stops, but the meaning goes on." He argued that in order to achieve the greatest possible effects on the reader through diversity, it would be desirable to use *hsing* and *pi* (which means "to express one's mind through objects"), alternatively, with the somewhat superficial mode of *fu*, as he considered *hsing* and *pi* as having more depth in meaning.[13]

Chung Hung's definition of *hsing* contradicts a basic etymological definition of the word as *beginning* (where the writing has just started). On the other hand, it agrees with the dominant sense of the term as a way to stir up emotions. Chung Hung's emphasis on something beyond the written text, however, is perhaps the earliest reference in Chinese literary criticism to the value of leaving room in the text for the reader's exploration. This value is highly relevant to our discussion of scenic closure, and will be brought up again later.

Chu Hsi attempted to give more concise and precise definitions of these terms respectively. While he was conversant with the discussion of these terms in the exegesis of the Confucian classics, Chu Hsi seemed to have never taken seriously the comments made by the literary critics of the Six Dynasties period. He explained *fu* as direct representation of the occasion or the event, *pi* as the use of one thing to describe another, and *hsing* as a mode in which one starts by talking about something else first before bringing out the subject matter of the text.[14]

From the above pastiche of earlier interpretations, we may understand the triad as a set of expressive modes that derived from the exegetical tradition of the *Shih-ching*, among which *hsing* will be our chief concern in this study, not only because it is the most ambiguous and controversial one, but also because it is the most relevant one to our topic. To achieve a better understanding of the term, let us examine in the following some of the *Shih-ching* texts traditionally considered to be examples of the use of *hsing*.

Both Liu Hsieh and Chu Hsi agreed with *Mao's Scholia* in picking out the song of *Ospreys* (*Kuan-chü*), the first poem in the *Shih-ching*, as an illustration of the use of *hsing*:

Kuan! Kuan! cry the ospreys
on the islet of the river;
The graceful and chaste maid—
a fair mate for our sire.

Long and short the water lily
to be picked left and right,
The graceful and chaste maid
He seeks, asleep or awake.

Seeking—but reaching her not,
awake or asleep He pines for her;
Long, for ever so long,
He tosses and turns around.

Long and short the water lily
to be culled left and right:
The graceful and chaste maid
to be wooed with lute and zither.

Long and short the water lily
to be plucked left and right:
The graceful and chaste maid
to be cheered with bell and drum.[15]

Having been liberated from the shackles of the rigid hermeneutics of the *Mao's Scholia*, a modern reader can well appreciate the poem in its own right. It is a lyric song of courtship, a poem about the perennial and perpetual subject matter of love. Like most primitive poetry intended for music, as most of the *Shih-ching* texts were, it has a repetitive structure.[16] Lines 3–4 are repeated, with some slight variation, in lines 7–8, 15–16, and 19–20. Lines 5–6 are repeated, with the variation of only one word in the line (*picked, culled, plucked*), in lines 13–14 and 17–18. In its overall structure the poem follows an underlying sequential order from thought to action, one that starts from a private one-sided adoration to the action, or at least the suggestion or anticipation of the action, of actual courtship.

What is noted in *Mao's Scholia* as an example of the use of *hsing* in this poem is at its beginning: the onomatopoeic representation of the ospreys (*chü chiu*: probably *pandion haliaetus*), something apparently unrelated to the subject of the human lovers. The beginning describes the sound of nature and evokes an image of birds, the river, the islet, initiated in the reiterated characters "Kuan! Kuan!"—onomatopoeia of the water-birds' crying. In what way is the sound related with the lovelorn man tossing and turning around in his bed? In what way is the picking of the water lily, repeatedly mentioned at the beginnings of the second, fourth, and fifth stanzas, related to the central theme of courtship?

Today one may have many reasons to be skeptical about the traditional exegeses, by which many texts in the *Shih-ching*, obviously love songs or songs about daily life, have been distorted beyond common sense. Even so, it is still often worthwhile to suspend our disbelief and try to make some critical use of them, as they can still provide a map of reference by which we learn associations and allusions in these ancient texts. In the case of this poem, traditional scholia cite an "old saying" (*chiu shuo*), which of course could well be just a pretext, that the ospreys are exemplary mates that remain loyal to each other. If one dies, the other follows from sadness. They are said to have an intimate but decent sexual relation. Hence, according to the ethical and historical commentary in *Mao's Scholia*, the use of the ospreys fits well with the theme of the noble virtues of the wives of King Chou Wen-wang, who remained loyal and decently affectionate to the sovereign (*chün-tzu*: "sire").

To a modern reader this may sound too much like what John Ruskin called "pathetic fallacy"—the imposition of human emotions, values, or characteristics on natural things, but a subtle association may still be traced using it as a point of departure. For example, the crying of these water-birds may be indicative of their period of sexual excitement in spring. Flowing by the islet where these ospreys stay is the river, which in the texts of the *Feng* section frequently stands for a barrier that one has to cross over to reach the beloved. Do not these natural signs of life and activity provide an agreeable background, a congenial ambience, for an amorous song as such? In fact, the use of the reiterated words at the beginning of the poem has been understood as the male and female birds, naturally corresponding to men and women, calling out to each other in a duet.[17]

On first look the picking of the water lily, a recurrent image in the poem, seems to have no more relation to the subject matter than the crying of the ospreys; but let us examine it more carefully. The origin of primitive music had much to do with collective labor or community ritual, so the action could be something the singers of this song were doing at the moment. As is illustrated in quite a number of other *Shih-ching* texts, just as in the folk song traditions of many different cultures from both East and West, the action of picking budding flowers often serves as a symbol of engaging a female in her prime in a love affair. The picking of the water lily (probably *nymphoides peltatum*), a pretty water-plant with bright yellow flowers, the leaves of which are said to be highly edible, may therefore be associated to the yearning of the sire for his "graceful and chaste" sweetheart.

The juxtaposition of natural and human activities in the poem helps to create a connection between its imagery and theme. For example, towards the end of the song the human music (*lute and zither, bell and drum*) takes the place of the music of nature, just as the rites of courtship with the sire and the maid as social beings (as suggested in the process of wooing and cheering with these musical instruments) replace the initial statement of longing and desire with the humans as natural beings.

Thus, although the images at the beginning of and throughout the poem seem at first sight to be unrelated to the theme, they begin to make sense in the reading process, as a close exploration brings in light traces of associations between the lines.

The *Shih-ching* abounds in similar use of scenic beginning. Here are just a few more examples of such use, traditionally considered to be examples of the application of *hsing*:

Lush, lush, the peach tree!
Its blossoms all ablaze;
This maid goes where she belongs—
A blessing to her house. (No. 6)

Tight, tight, the hare-net,
Ding! ding! it is set.
Burly are these fighting men—
Fort and shield to our lords. (No. 7)

A rainbow is in the east,
None dares to point to it;
The young woman is going away,
Far from her parents and brothers. (No. 51)

Look yon the bay of the river,
The green bamboos are so lush!
Graceful is our lord—
As if carved, as if filed,
As if chiseled, as if polished,
Grave and solemn,
Radiant and lofty,

Graceful is our lord,
Not to be forgot. (No. 55)

In the wild the crawling grass
Is all covered with dropping dew.
There is a beautiful one
With eyes and brows so pretty;
All by chance we encountered,
I gained what I wanted. (No. 94)

In all these passages, the opening images have no apparent links with subsequent lines that generally lay out the theme of the poem. On a close examination, however, as in the case of the song of *Ospreys*, associations can be established, as have often been achieved in traditional criticism.

Thus, for example, in No. 6 (*T'ao-yao*), apparently a song of blessing at a young woman's wedding day, the visual image of the peach flowers parallels one of the bride. In our time the use of flowers as symbols for females is so common that one almost takes it for granted. Still one may ask: how did it initially work out? The association in this text seems to establish itself on certain points of generality:

Peach = flowering, luxuriant
(explicit, as stated in the text by "Lush, lush")

Bride = in the prime of youth and beauty
(implicit, suggested by the association)

Though the two objects are different (plant versus human being), they converge on two aspects: first, they are both in the prime of their life duration; second, they are both pleasing to the eye in their beauty. These qualities of the latter are not stated in the text, they are called forth by the parallel image of the former. The peach is a very common plant found over a vast area of China, that usually flowers in the peak of spring (a season for sowing and planting as well as for love and mating). In the second line of the next two stanzas, the word "blossoms" is replaced by "fruit" and "leaves" in turn. Does the order suggest, in a subtle way, the prospective events of the next stages in the bride's life: pregnancy and procreation? This poem was among the earliest Chinese literary texts that established the bright-colored and luxuriant peach flowers as a set symbol for young women.

In No. 7 (*T'u-chü*), an eulogy of feudal warriors, the relation between the opening image (the hare-net being set up in the forest) and the subject of the text (men of arms who serve as bodyguards for aristocrats) is rather dubious. It is certainly possible that these warriors were actually engaged in the action of setting up a hare-net, not unlikely in a hunting trip, in which case the beginning imagery may also be regarded as in the mode of *fu*, that of direct presentation or description of the actual scene. It has generally been suggested that the relation between the beginning and the subject of this poem is to be traced in the reiterated modifier ("Tight, tight"). Just as the hare-net, tightly set up, would not allow its prey to escape, the warriors, tightly disciplined, would keep any enemy from getting through to their lord. It was probably on the basis of such an observation that Chu Hsi picked out this text, along with the song of *Ospreys*, as representative of the use of *hsing*.

It is even more difficult to ascertain the relation between the opening image of the rainbow and the subject matter of the young woman leaving her family in No. 51 (*Ti-tung*). One old Chinese interpretation goes as follows. As the rainbow is seen in the west in the morning and in the east in the afternoon (change of opposite directions within a day). it has become a symbol for infidelity, fickleness, or sexual misconduct. From such an association, there developed the historical exegesis that the poem was meant as a satire against Duke Hsüan-kung of the Wei, who contracted a young lady from the dukedom of Ch'i by the name of Chiang to marry his son, but, on seeing her, seized her and made her his own concubine. Thus the poem has been traditionally taken as a defense of Chiang, who was forced into an awkward and improper relationship. One may well choose to ignore such historical allusions and, following the general idea that the rainbow is a sign of the evil force and of bad omen, regard the opening image as a bad omen for ill fortune to the young lady who was separated from her own family.[18] If so, one should note an important difference here. In the previous examples, even if one excludes historical interpretation, the reading of the images would still demonstrate the propriety of these images to the main theme. In the case of this poem, such an a-historical reading would actually change the interpretation of the main theme entirely.

The scenic beginning in No. 55 (*Ch'i-yü*) was the earliest example of what was to become a conventional association between bamboo and men of great virtue and knowledge. Although the basic association is made here, it is interesting to note that its elaboration, those qualities of the bamboo that correspond to the qualities of the virtuous scholar, differs from later times. Here, its pleasing green color, its denseness and luxuriance seem to be the qualities roughly transferred to the human situation. Later, the bamboo would come to be associated with unswerving loyalty not to be bent by force (because of its firmness and straightness), probably from the related word *chieh*, the joints of the bamboo which also means integrity. Bamboo was even personified as a peer gentleman, the perfect companion of a man of letters.

No. 94 (*Yeh yu man-ts'ao*) is about love at first sight. The grass in the wild, fresh and luxuriant, parallels the beautiful one, young and glamorous. The dew, that provides sustenance and nourishment for the grass, may suggest, in a subtle way, the act of love and its satisfaction ("I gained what I wanted").

From these examples, and from the numerous discussions of that triad of poetic terms mentioned above, I shall venture to explain *hsing* as, first of all, a mode of expression that uses concrete images of objects (*wu*), those that are external to the speaker's mind but nevertheless appeal to his senses (auditory, visual, tactile, etc.), in order to evoke, through indirect and often subtle associations, the subject of the poem, and bring it into a certain perspective.

Because of the subtlety and indirectness of the associations, the significance of *hsing* lies hidden in a poetic text, waiting to be explored, found, and appreciated in the reading process. The use of *hsing* helps to expand the semantic and interpretative dimensions of the text. In this sense it bears some resemblance to *conceit*, a term of the Metaphysical Poets, which is defined (in *The Oxford English Dictionary*) as "far-fetched comparison or euphemism."[19] One difference, however, is that while the *conceit* is composed as an constructed association for the reader's interpretation and appreciation of its complexity, there is a strong sense of improvisation and immediacy about *hsing*, an organic and natural, if frequently mysterious, correspondence, as if the images were something the poet or the singer actually heard or saw while composing these texts.

Last but not the least, *hsing* is, from its etymological meaning, closely related with poetic beginning. What have been critically attributed to be its uses in the *Shih-ching* texts primarily occur at the beginning, either of the whole poem, or of one or all (in repetition) of its stanzas. To present concrete images to open a text, or "to raise the topic by means of objects" (*t'o wu ch'i hsing*), is not only a basic pattern of the *Shih-ching*, but has also become one of the structural principles of Chinese poetry ever since. The use of *hsing* also accounts for the fact that the beginning often stands as the dominant part in the structure of early Chinese poetic texts.

If *hsing* is primarily used at the beginning of the *Shih-ching* texts, then how about their closure? Before we try to find an answer for this question, it is necessary to first consider larger questions of structure, i.e., the ways in which semantic elements are arranged in lines and stanzas of the *Shih-ching* poems.

A survey of the anthology's 305 pieces reveals two basic structural types: the *parallel* or *paratactic* structure, and the *linear* or *sequential* structure. A great majority of the 160 texts in the *Feng* section, more than half of the 74 texts in the *Hsiao-ya* section, and about half a dozen among the 31 texts of the *Ta-ya* section, belong to the first type. These texts consist of two or more stanzas which, in terms of their contents, do not follow a sequential order, but are semantically parallel to one another. The diction among the stanzas is often repetitive, with some variation in characters. The stanzas of these poems can be re-arranged without bringing about any substantial change of the contents and meaning of the whole. One example of this is the beautiful love song, No. 129 (*Chien-chia*):

The young reeds are lush, so lush,
The white dew becomes frost;
He who I call "that one"
Is on the side of the river.
I go up the stream in his wake,
The way is hard and long;
I go down the stream after him—
He seems to be in the midst of the water.

The young reeds are dense, so dense,
The white dew is not dried up yet;
He who I call "that one"
Is on the bank of the river.
I go up the stream in his wake,
The way is hard and steep;
I go down the stream after him—
He seems to be on an islet in the water.

The young reeds are thick, so thick,
The white dew is still on;
He who I call "that one"
Is on the brink of the river.

I go up the stream in his wake,
The way is hard and winding;
I go down the stream after him—
He seems to be on an isle in the water.

There is no clear linear semantic development in the text. One may even shift the order of the three stanzas bringing about little, if any, alteration in the meaning of the entire poem.

The rest of the poems in the three sections, which consists of a minority in overall proportion (though a majority in the *Ta-ya* section), and the entirety of the 39 hymns in the *Sung* section, possess a linear structure that presents a sequence of events or a process of action throughout the text. The most obvious examples in such structure are the shorter historical ballads in the *Ta-ya* section, such as No. 236 (*Ta-ming*), No. 237 (*Mien*), No. 241 (*Huang-yi*), No. 245 (*Sheng-min*), and No. 250 (*Kung Liu*). These are all stories about the early ancestors of the Chou dynasty: their military campaigns, their farming activities, and even an exodus.

In between these two basic types, some short lyric songs in the *Feng* section, although they consist of apparently recurrent stanzas, nevertheless reveal an underlying linear structure in a subtle way. The song of *Ospreys*, for example, belongs to such a mixed type, because the repetitions and variations of its stanzas somehow suggest a temporal sequence, one that starts from a kind of one-sided lovelorn thoughts, and develops towards an open courtship ("woos with lute and zither") and even consummation ("cheers with drum and bell"). Many texts of this middle type begin exactly like those in parallel structure, but change either half way in the poem, or sometimes in the last stanza. One example of this is No. 13 (*Ts'ai-fan*):

Whither to pick aster?
In the pond, on the islets.
Whither to apply it?
At the ritual of our lords.

Whither to pick aster?
In the mountain streams.
Whither to apply it?
In the temple of our lords.

How rich is the ornament!
Dawn till dusk they are at the rites.

How profuse is the ornament!
Here they are on their way home.

This song gives an account of a company of noblewomen, richly ornamented, engaging themselves with the preparation and performance of religious services, probably of ancestral worship. While the first and second stanzas keep a parallel structure, like most songs in the *Feng* section, the third stanza turns the poem into one of linear structure, since there reveals a clear suggestion about the proceeding ("Dawn till dark") and the closure ("on their way home") of the ritual. This combination of parallel structure (usually in the first two or several stanzas) and linear structure (mostly in the last stanza or in the latter half of the poem) is typical of a number of texts in the *Feng* and *Hsiao-ya* sections. However, these poems incline towards the linear type, as it is the linear stanza that changes and dominates the overall structure of the entire text.

There is also another variation which, despite its recurrent structure and overall pattern of repetition, nevertheless keeps an order of gradation in its stanzas. The song of blessing for the bride cited above (No. 6), in which the word *blossoms* in the first stanza is replaced by *fruit* and *leaves* in the next two stanzas respectively, is one of the four songs in the anthology that hold such a structure. Here are the first stanzas of the other three songs which, like No. 6, all belong to the *Feng* section:

The plums drop,
There are seven of them;
Those men who seek after me,
The time for it is good. (No. 20)

He is picking the mugwort—
Missing him for one day
Is like three months long! (No. 72)

He waits for me at the gate, aha,
His ear-plugs use white strings, aha,
And over them are fine jewels, aha! (No. 98)

The first of these, No. 20 (*Piao yu mei*), is the closest in essence among early Chinese poems to European lyric songs in the motif of *carpe diem*.[20] The second line of the first stanza, a simple statement about the condition of the plums, has its variation in the next two stanzas as "There are three of them" and "They are all picked into the basket."

The plum tree, shedding its ripe fruit, becomes a counterpart of the growing maturity of the young lady, the speaker in the poem who calls upon her wooers to make haste, lest the prime of her beauty be gone. The variation of the second line through the stanzas bring about an increasing sense of the pressing time, and of the fleeting youth and beauty.

In No. 72 (*Ts'ai-ko*), another short love song of three stanzas, the hyperbolic simile "like three months long" in the first stanza is replaced respectively by "like three autumns long" and "like three years long" in the next two stanzas. Although there is no actual progression in meaning, the order of the variables, each representing a longer duration of time (month, season, year), creates a sense of growing intensity.

No. 98 (*Chu*) is probably about a bride peeping at the bridegroom, presumably from behind the curtain in the main hall, when he comes to pick her up on the wedding day. Here the gradation is a spatial one: the expression "at the gate" in the first stanza is replaced by "in the courtyard" and "in the hall" in the second and third stanza. While variations of other characters among the stanzas, such as words of the color of the ear-plug strings (white / green / yellow), are parallel in their meanings, the variation of the spatial terms does indicate the shortening distance between the bride and the approaching bridegroom.

The structural patterns of the *Shih-ching* texts can be represented by the following diagrams:

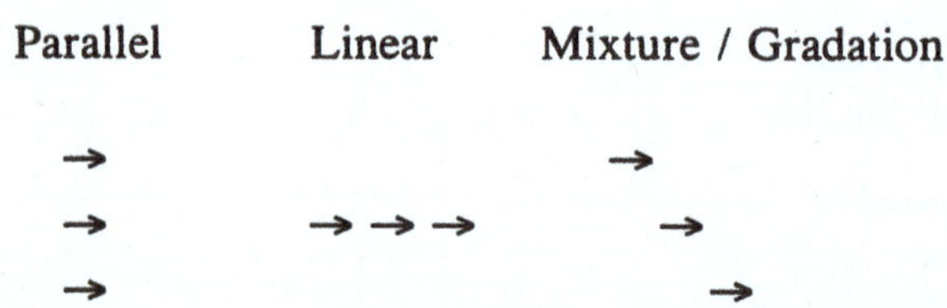

Because of the repetitive format and the absence of a sequential order, poems of parallel structure usually do not have a very clear sense of closure. Let us compare the closure of No. 13 and No. 129, both of which have been discussed in the above. In the former the last line "Here they are on their way home," clearly suggests the termination of the ceremony, and accordingly a termination of the action as well as the poem itself. The last line of the latter, "He seems to be on the isle in the water," does not progress any further than the last lines of the two previous stanzas in sequential order; the poem can well stop at the end of the second stanza, or simply goes on for a few more stanzas, as long as the singer can find synonyms to substitute words like "islet" or "isle."

In short, a poem of linear structure usually closes at the end of the last line, a line that often refers to the unfolding, developing, or proceeding of an event or an action as presented by the poem. A poem of parallel structure, on the other hand, closes where it does for no apparent reasons. Still, our ancient singers found different ways of bringing a song to a close, and consciously or unconsciously on their part, found different ways to give the reader a sense of this act of closing. Indeed a survey of the *Shih-ching* reveals the full range of basic closure patterns found in the later development of Chinese poetry.

In the *Shih-ching* texts, the most common way of conferring a sense of closure to a text, particularly one in parallel structure, is to break the repetitive pattern by introducing a final stanza that does not repeat the beginning lines of previous stanzas. In No. 13, as discussed above, it is the last stanza that breaks the paratactic pattern of the two previous stanzas, and this change in form is further accentuated by semantic suggestions which bring the poem to a conclusion. The two do not always work together; often the sense of closure is brought about primarily through prosodic means. Such is the case with No. 42 (*Ching-nü*), the song about a love rendezvous:

A quiet lady, oh she's pretty,
Is to see me at the corner of the citadel.
I love her, and seeing her not,
I scratch my head, and loiter around.

A quiet lady, oh she's lovely,
Presents me with a red pipe.
The red pipe has a lustre;
How I delight in thy beauty.

From the mead she brings sprouts
That are truly beautiful and rare.
'Tis not that they are really beautiful:
But they are given me by a beauty.

In this song, unlike many *Shih-ching* texts with set patterns of repetition through to the end, the third stanza drops the phrase "A quiet lady" at the beginning. In the original, the number of Chinese words in each line forms the pattern 4–5–4–4 / 4–4–4–4 / 4–4–5–4. Lines 2 and

11 are both pentasyllabic lines while all the rest are tetrasyllabic lines, thus giving the poem a kind of symmetry. One may argue that the last two lines here contain conclusive elements in the reaffirmation of her beauty. Still it is the formal change in the third stanza that highlights this closing statement.

For poems in linear structure the closure is often enforced by formal changes in the last stanza, such as in No. 23 (*Yeh yu ssu-chün*):

In the wild is a dead doe
Wrapped up in white rushes;
A maid yearns for springtime
For a handsome man to seduce.

In the woods there are shrubs,
In the wild is a dead deer
Bound up in white rushes;
A maid there is—fair as jade.

"Easy, hey, gently, gently!
Touch not, hey, my waistcloth!
And don't make the dog bark!"

In this song, while the first and second stanzas are in parallel structure, the last stanza again deviates from the pattern, and the alteration is manifold. In the original, the tetrasyllabic quatrain of the first two stanzas changes to the pentasyllabic triplet of the last stanza. The speaker in the last stanza is no longer the omniscient narrator, but shifts to the maid herself, described in the earlier stanzas. The figure of thought also turns into the use of direct speech, what the Roman rhetorician Quintilian called *apostrophe*—a digression in discourse, a turning away from an audience to address an imaginary person. Through the formal change and the rhetorical effects, the poem is brought to a conclusion indicative of the development in relation from courtship to intimacy.

Besides those employing formal changes, as we have just discussed above, the most common type of closure is a declaration of what is in the speaker's mind. In most stanzaic texts in the anthology, one may notice a movement within each of the stanzas, from the objects (*wu*) cited at the beginning, to a statement of feeling or a sense of the self (*wo*) of the speaker. Such a movement on the stanzaic level is also reflected in most cases on the level of the entire text.[21] This type of closing with a statement of the self may be further categorized as follows in terms of their various figures of mood or thought.

a. Lamenting:

Have the chaise ready, take a trip
To drive out the sorrow in my heart. (No. 39)

Have the boat ready, take a voyage,
To drive out the sorrow in my heart. (No. 59)

I want my man, I miss him,
It inflicts pain on my heart. (No. 62)

b. Questioning (often in the form of "rhetorical questions"):

It is really the Heaven's doing,
What can one say about it? (No. 40)

That handsome gentleman,
What should I tell him? (No. 53)

Those who know me
    think I am sad in heart;
Those who know me not
    wonder what I want.
Oh blue Heaven far above,
Who is to blame for that? (No. 65)

Oh my heart, oh my heart,
In what month shall I return? (No. 68)

c. Swearing / Emotional Exclamation:

Till death, I swear, I won't change,
Oh mother, oh heaven,
Thou understand me not! (No. 45)

Since he looks back not on old times—
Then just let it rest! (No. 58)

Oh how blue is that Heaven
That kills our good men!
If only they could be redeemed—
A hundred people for each of them! (No. 131)

d. Imperative / Wishful:

Trusty is my lord,
Come back, oh, come back! (No. 19)

My lord is on an expedition,
May he hunger and thirst not! (No. 66)

May he take care of himself,
So that he may return, and die not! (No. 110)

e. Reflective:

In the mountains are lacquer trees,
Chestnut trees are in the low land.
Now that you have wine and food,
Why not play your zither every day?
Have fun with it and be merry,
Use it to prolong the day.
By the time you breathe your last,
Others will take your place. (No. 115)

A number of songs in the anthology have a kind of closure that refers to the purpose of the composing of the text, which may be called the meta-poetic closure:

This is meant as a taunt. (No. 107)

Therefore I wrote this song
To convey my thoughts of mother. (No. 162)

I have made this nice song
To explore your fickle mind. (No. 199)

A nobleman has made the song
So that his woe be heard. (No. 204)

A few poems are presented
To be made into songs. (No. 252)

There is also a type of closure in the form of words of blessing which was perhaps used conventionally by musicians or singers at the end of singing, such as in the following:

Holding up goblets of rhinoceros horns:
"A long, long life of countless years!" (No. 154)

To be rewarded with great blessing,
And a long, long life of countless years. (No. 210 / No. 211)

If we consider the closure of the *Shih-ching* texts in the light of the triad of *fu*, *pi*, and *hsing*, then the different types of endings above (be it statement of mind, reference to the composing itself, or words of blessing) may be regarded as examples of the application of *fu*, the unfigured direct exposition.

There are poems that use the mode of *pi* at closure. There are only a few of these, but in them the concluding similes or metaphors give a particular force to their closure:

Burly are these fighting men—
Belly and heart to our lords. (No. 7)

My heart is rueful
Like an unwashed dress;
Reflecting upon it in the still—
If only I could fly up and away! (No. 26)

You think I am not to be trusted?
But I am like the bright sun! (No. 73)

The lady of Ch'i goes where she belongs,
Her escort is like flowing water. (No. 104)

Scary and wary—
As if on the brink of a deep pool,
As if treading upon thin ice. (No. 195)

In No. 26 (*Po-chou*), a female persona voices her anxiety and suffering for being forced to do something against her own will, and for being humiliated and insulted by the "petty ones." It may well be a political satire of the perennial theme of "disused talent" (*huai ts'ai pu yü*), according to the interpretation in *Mao's Scholia*. The closure, evoking the image of a bird that can flap its wings and fly away freely, intensifies the speaker's discontent with her surroundings, and her yearning for another world afar that may prove different from the world in which she finds herself. The final vow in No. 73 (*Ta-chü*), made more vivid by the simile, gives a decisive conclusion to the whole poem, which is probably an exchange of vows between lovers. In No. 195 (*Hsiao-min*), obviously a political satire, the closure summarizes in vivid images all the hidden danger and risk of court service. The use of figurative language endows such endings with no less force than that of the *hsing* beginning of many poems in the anthology.

There is a very small group of poems in the anthology that use the mode of *hsing* at closure to great effect. The late Professor Hsü Fu-kuan, developing Chung Hung's definition of *hsing* as the mode in which "the writing stops but the meaning goes on," has argued that there are certain anomalies among the *Shih-ching* texts, in which the use of *hsing* has shifted its position from the beginning to the middle or the ending of a stanza. According to him, the shifting of the position of the *hsing*, as well as the combination of all three modes, signifies a development from simple, naive forms to complex, sophisticated forms. Only when the *hsing* is placed at the ending of a poem, he further observes, does its use reach its consummation.[22] The example he cited for illustration of such an accomplished use of *hsing* is No. 117 (*Chiao-liao*):

The fruits of prickly ash
Grow and spread, filling a pint.
That man over there
Is so big, with no match.
Oh prickly ash!
Oh spreading far!

The fruits of prickly ash
Grow and spread, filling my hands.
That man over there
Is so big and strong.
Oh prickly ash!
Oh spreading far!

The Chinese prickly ash (*chiao*: probably *zanthoxylum bungeanum*) is a plant noted for its fertility. Since the poem has been generally understood as a song of blessing for a bride who is probably large in physique, traditionally believed to be a good sign for her reproductive power, the reference to the prickly ash therefore symbolizes the prospect of prosperity for her family and descendants. The last two lines repeat the beginning image, that of the fruits of the plant spreading far and wide, but they take the form of an interjection of admiration on the part of the speaker, emphasizing the luxuriance of the plant. Such an auditory exclamation, as Professor Hsü has observed, gives the whole text at its end a lingering emotional effect that exemplifies Chung Hung's description of *hsing*.

Professor Hsü did not provide any further illustration of such use of *hsing* at closure. There are indeed not too many of such "anomalies." A rare example using visual image at the stanzaic closure is No. 140 (*Tung-meng chih yang*):

> The poplar tree at East Gate,
> Its leaves rustle and rustle;
> Due to meet at dusk:
> The Bright Star twinkles.
>
> The poplar tree at East Gate,
> Its leaves rustle and rustle;
> Due to meet at dusk:
> The Bright Star glitters.

This poem tells about a man waiting for his beloved at a rendezvous ("the East Gate"). Throughout the poem, nothing is stated explicitly about his mind. It is chiefly through what he hears (the rustling of the poplar tree) and what he sees (the twinkling of the star), through the contrast of the appointed time (dusk) and the suggested "present" time (the star is twinkling and glittering), that all the anxiety and anticipation of waiting for the loved one are suggested in a covert, implicit way. The closure, indicative of a temporal distance between the appointed hour and the narrative present of the song, plays an important role in the structure.[23]

A truly remarkable and singular use of scenic closure in the *Shih-ching* occurs, it seems to me, in the last poem of the *Hsiao-ya* section, No. 234 (*Ho ts'ao pu huang*):

> What grass turns not yellow?
> What day is not set for march?
> What man tramps not in file,
>   and be engaged in four directions?
>
> What grass turns not black?
> What man feels not bereaved?
> Alas for us men on service—
>   as if we alone were not fellow beings!

Behold those rhinos, and those tigers,
roaming about the wilds;
Alas for us men on service—
day and night, moving for ever!

A fox with a fluffy tail
trots along deep in grass;
Carriages lofty and grand
move along the highways.

This poem has an unusually complex structure. The first two stanzas are primarily parallel ones, but a progression is already revealed as the questioning in lines 3–4 of the first stanza turns into the sorrowful exclamation in lines 7–8 of the second stanza. The third stanza breaks the parallel pattern in its first two lines, but it is linked to the previous stanza by the repetition of line 7 in line 11. The fourth and last stanza then abruptly turns away from the emotional interjection in previous stanzas to a pair of visual images at which the poem closes.

The poem starts with three successive questions. The use of *anaphora* in the first stanza, the deliberate repetition of the word "What" (*ho*) at the beginning of three successive lines, intensifies the force of painful doubt in the speaker's mind. Chu Hsi has pointed out that the beginning of this poem is an example of the use of *hsing*: the grass in the wild, turning yellow in autumn and withering away ("black") in winter, may be associated with the campaigning men in the poem, languishing in toil and fatigue. The image of wild animals at the beginning of the third stanza also draws a parallel with the men, who, as suggested at the end of the second stanza, are not well treated, but rather are forced to march forward against their own will, in an expedition as purposeless to them as the roaming in the wild of those rhinos and tigers.

The fourth and last stanza, forming a sharp contrast with all three previous stanzas, is one devoid of any verbal comment or lament, and yet rich in all its suggestiveness. Poetry reading often demands an extension of one's "inward eye" from what is overt and implicit in the text to what is covert or implicit there. In this stanza, the speaker himself and his fellow men are not even mentioned, but they are nevertheless ever present behind the description of the scene. These poor wayfarers can neither be like the fox, moving freely on its own, or presumably back to its own lair; nor can they ride the lofty and grand carriages like the aristocrats. The reader is led to see the images exactly as the speaker might have seen them, and to muse on what might have gone through the speaker's mind.

In other words, the last stanza is set for contrast, for throwing the misery of the speaker and his fellow travellers into strong relief. While the speaker seems to be openly lamenting in the first stanzas, he withholds himself from any outcry of grievance and complaint in the last stanza, leaving the images to speak for themselves. "At this moment, silence excels any sound," to quote Po Chü-yi's line from his *Song of the P'i-p'a*. I shall venture to argue that this is an even more fully developed illustration of concluding *hsing* than Professor Hsü's example, No. 117. The switch from thought to scene gives this poem a dynamism, and the meaning of the poem really extends beyond its closure. However, compared to the majority of *Shih-ching* texts, poems like these are really "anomalies." But this last example fully deserves to be considered as a forerunner of those great Tu Fu poems using scenic closure. With this and the other examples, the *Shih-ching* remains, like all great early literary works in other cultures, to be the source of inspiration that has provided a great variety of patterns for later generations.

Notes

1. This is from the poem *Presented to the Honorable Vice Minister Wei: A Poem in 22 Rhymed Couplets* (2251–52). Just to give a few more examples here, with all words referring to the word *shen* (translated as *divinity* or *gods*) italicized: "I just feel that there stand spirits and *gods* while singing loudly" (*Song Written in Drunkenness*, 2257); "In the darkness, my feelings are raised by *divinity*" (*Presented to Vice Minister Wei: 20 Rhymed Couplets*, 2389); "His writing has *divinity* in it, and he is good at making friends" (*Song Written in Drunkenness for Hsüeh Hua at a Banquet given by Su Tuan and Hsüeh Fu*, 2270); "When the poem is completed, I feel as if it were done by *divinity*" (*A Poem Written while Drinking Alone*, 2407); "The stimulation (*hsing*) of poetry is not without *divinity*" (*Mailed to Chang Piao the Mountain Recluse in 30 Rhymed Couplets*, 2429); "When his brush is put down, wind and rain arise / When his poem is finished, spirits and *gods* weep" (*Presented to Li Po in 20 Rhymed Couplets*, 2430). All page numbers of Tu Fu texts, given parenthetically as in the previous chapter, are from *Chüan T'ang shih*, VII.

2. This remark is from Huang T'ing-chien's letter addressed to his nephew Hung Chü-fu. See Kuo and Wang, II, p. 316. For an English rendition of a part of that letter see Palumbo-Liu, p. 66.

3. I have no intention to give a full treatment of this triad of modes in my study.

Instead I shall concentrate on the issue in the context of poetic beginning and poetic closure only in my discussion. The bulk of related scholarship in Chinese has been upsurging ever since the Han dynasty, and since the Ch'ing dynasty has become diabolically intimidating. One of the earlier discussion of this issue in English (and in my opinion still one of the best) was done by the late Professor Shih-hsiang Chen (1912–71). See his article "The *Shih-ching*: Its Generic Significance in Chinese Literary History and Poetics," in Cyril Birch ed., *Studies in Chinese Literary Genres* (Berkeley: university of California Press, 1974), pp. 8–41. For more comprehensive discussion of the triad of modes see Steven Van Zoeren, *Poetry and Personality: Reading, Exegesis, and Hermeneutics in Traditional China* (Stanford: Stanford University Press, 1991) and Pauline Yu, *The Reading of Imagery in the Chinese Tradition* (Princeton: Princeton University, 1987).

4. Kuo and Wang, I, pp. 63–69. For a complete translation with extensive commentary and critical notes see Owen, *Readings*, pp. 37–49, especially pp. 45–46.

5. Cited in Kuo and Wang, I, p. 68.

6. K'ung Ying-ta, *Mao-Shih cheng-i*, *chüan* 1. Cited in Kuo and Wang, I, p. 68.

7. Chu Hsi, *Chu-tzu yü-lei*, ed. by Li Ching-te, new punctuated edition by Wang Hsing-mao (Peking: Chung-hua shu-chü, 8 Vols., 1986), VI, pp. 2069–70.

8. One notable dissenting argument is that of Huang Ch'e, a twelfth century scholar who maintained that *feng, ya* and *sung* in the context of the "Six Principles" are not the same as those used as names for the three sections of the *Shih-ching*. His interpretation, strongly morality-oriented, is that *feng* is to move and inspire, *ya* is to rectify what goes wrong, and *sung* is to glorify. Huang was nevertheless not at loggerheads with the traditional definitions of the other triad. Cited in Wei Ch'ing-chih ed. *Shih-jen yü-hsüeh* (Shanghai: Ku-chi ch'u-pan-she, 2 Vols., 1978), I, p. 268.

9. From K'ung Ying-ta, *Mao-Shih cheng-yi* in the *Shih-san-ching chu-shu*. Cited in Chao Chih-yang, *Shih-ching fu-pi-hsing chung-lun* (Hsin-chu: Feng-ch'eng ch'u-pan-she, 1974), p. 29.

10. Kuo and Wang, I, pp. 190–205.

11. From Chu Hsi, *Ssu-shu chi-chu*, *Lun-yü* (*Analects*), XVII (*Yang Ho* 9), p. 121.

12. Liu Hsieh, pp. 394–403. For a complete translation of this chapter with critical notes see Owen, *Readings*, pp. 256–62.

13. Kuo and Wang, I, pp. 308–23. Also see Chapter 1, note 2.

14. Chu Hsi, *Chu-tzu yü-lei*, VI, pp. 2069–70.

15. See *Bibliography* for all the books consulted on the *Shih-ching*. For the basic text I used *Mao-Shih* (Reprint of the *Ssu-pu pei-yao* Edition, Shanghai: Chung-hua shu-chü, 4 Vols. Undated). Occasional specific citations from both Chinese and Western sources will be credited in notes. All English translations of the *Shih-ching* texts, unless specifically noted, are mine.

16. A few scholars, including Ku Yen-wu, have argued, without much cogent evidence, that not all the *Shih-ching* texts were originally set in music. From many references to the *Shih* in classic texts such as the *Yüeh-chi* (*Notes on Music*), the *Li-chi* (*Book of Rites*), the *Yi-wen chih* (*Record of Literature and Arts*), the *Han-shu* (*History of the Han*), etc., I advocate the theory that all the *Shih-ching* texts were set in music. See *Hsien-Ch'in wen-hsüeh-shih ts'an-k'ao tzu-liao*, ed. by the Teaching and Research Group of the History of Chinese Literature, Peking University (Peking: Chung-hua shu-

chü, 1962), pp. 128–31.

17. See the comment of Liu Yün-cheng, a Ch'ing scholar, cited in P'ei P'u-hsien ed. *Shih-ching p'ing-chu tu-pen* (Taipei: San-min shu-chü, 2 Vols., 1982), I, p. 4. Before him, Cheng Hsüan had defined "Kuan! Kuan!" as *ho sheng*, which may mean simultaneous utterance of different voices, or crying to each other in reply.

18. One example of free interpretation of this image was made by Arthur Waley, who gave full reins to his imagination in arguing that "the arc of the rainbow typifies the swelling girdle of a pregnant woman." See Waley, *The Book of Songs: The Ancient Chinese Classic of Poetry* (New York: Grove Press, 1987), p. 61.

19. See *The Oxford English Dictionary* (Oxford: Clarendon Press, Second Edition, 20 Vols., 1989), II. The Chinese *hsing*, however, does not necessarily carry with it a fanciful element as the metaphysical *conceit* usually does.

20. Although the Chinese motif of *chi shih hsing le* (to lose no time seeking pleasure) and the Western *carpe diem* both originated from a sense of the transiency of human life, especially that of youth and beauty, they developed on very different lines in later stages. While the Western *carpe diem* poetry evolved into *carpe rosem* poetry addressed to females, as represented, for example, by the poems of Ronsard or Marvell, the Chinese *chi shih hsing le* theme was often assimilated into drinking poems.

21. It should be noted here that in poems of parallel structure with no linear development in the text, the structure of the first stanza usually repeats itself in subsequent stanzas. The endings of the different stanzas can be exactly the same, or with some slight variation only. In such cases, the stanzaic ending is to be considered the ending of the text, even though there is no clear sense of closure in these texts.

22. See Hsü Fu-kuan's important article on the interpretation of *pi* and *hsing* in his *Chung-kuo wen-hsüeh lun-chi* (Taipei: Taiwan hsüeh-sheng shu-chü, Fifth Edition, 1985), pp. 91–117. For this argument see pp. 110–17.

23. I am unsure that this poem is about a *rendezvous manqué* (Ezra Pound's title for the poem), as most English translators have taken it to be. The temporal aspect of the poem is quite ambiguous. *Ming hsing* (Bright Star) is an archaic Chinese word for the planet Venus, which appears both at sunrise and during sometime after sunset, and is therefore not necessarily the "morning star" (as Arthur Waley and Bernhard Karlgren both put it), which means only the planet when it is visible in the east before sunrise. Neither Waley nor Karlgren seems to have been aware that there is a duration of twelve hours between dusk and dawn. It would make equal, if not better, sense if *ming hsing* is understood as the evening star. Although the girl is late in coming, the man has not yet lost his hope and he is still waiting. In my translation I have therefore tried to retain the ambiguity in the original.

4

Continuation and Variation: A Diachronic Survey of Poetic Closure Through the High T'ang

IN the millennium between the world of the *Shih-ching* and Tu Fu's age, Chinese poetry went through many phases of change, but the basic structural patterns of the *Shih-ching* texts, especially that of beginning with an image of external objects and closing with the expression of thought and emotion, continued with little variation. Yet, although poems from the ancient anthology were both commonly quoted and performed to music during the next several centuries following its compilation (generally believed to be in the 6th century B.C.), little new *shih* (poetry in the *Shih-ching* forms), if any, was preserved from that period.

The disintegration of the rites and music with the weakening and then the collapse of the royal Chou court, and the turmoil in the divided, war-ridden northern China, may have accounted for such dwindling of the *shih* poetry. Pan Ku, the great historian of the Western Han, gave a brief explanation of the phenomenon in the preface he wrote for his rhyme-prose expositions (*fu*) of the *Two Capitals* (*Liang ching fu*):

> When Ch'eng and K'ang passed away, the sound of the hymns died down, when the bounties of the royal house were exhausted, the songs (*shih*) were no longer sung.[1]

This certainly did not mean the decline of all literary forms during the period. On the contrary, non-fictional literary prose, for example, found varied and highly elaborated forms in the works of historians, philosophers, and educators. There also developed, in the third century B.C., the literary form of the *Ch'u-tz'u*, which had an independent evolution on its own, and became the formal and structural precursor of the rhyme-prose exposition (*fu*) that flourished during the Han dynasty.[2] The poetic form (mainly tetrasyllabic verse) of the *Shih-ching* texts never returned to a dominant position in Chinese literature, though the lyric essence of these poems found a new form in the *yüeh-fu* (Music Bureau) convention, which did not take place until the second century B.C, leaving in between a long interval of some four centuries.

During the Han dynasty the rhyme-prose exposition, the dominant literary genre of the period that had a more direct formal relation with the *Ch'u-tz'u*, flowed and surged like a great river, whereas the *shih*, the shorter, more personal lyric form of the *Shih-ching* tradition, gurgled like a little brook. It was nevertheless an age that saw the *shih* form evolve, with the old tetrasyllabic verse surviving primarily as a stiff, archaic form, supplanted by the new, popular pentasyllabic verse. The new form had occasionally been used in the folk verse, though often in a mixture with lines of variable length, as early as during the reign of the Ch'in empire in late third century B.C. It began to be more widely adopted, however, in the *yüeh-fu* songs. By the Eastern Han (the first to the early third century A.D.), it was firmly established as the major poetic form. The change of form marked a great leap in the development of Chinese poetry. Except in some song forms, the prosodic change from the tetrasyllabic line to the pentasyllabic line was also accompanied by a shift of dominance from stanzaic structure, found in most of the *Shih-ching* texts, to linear structure.

During the reign of the Martial Emperor (*Wu-ti*), the sixth and the most powerful ruler of the Han dynasty, a "Music Bureau" (*yüeh-fu*) was established by imperial order. Its multiple official function included the composition of music and song texts to be used in state ceremonies and imperial occasions such as banquets and outings, the collection of folk songs in the empire, and the training of court musicians. An institution by that name was known earlier during the previous Ch'in dynasty and also during the reign of Emperor Hui-ti (194–187 B.C.), but nothing from the *yüeh-fu* prior to the Martial Emperor reign remains extant today.[3] From the entire Han dynasty only about sixty odd folk songs from the Music Bureau collection have survived, and the majority of these songs belong to the Eastern Han period.[4]

In sharp contrast to the highly elaborate form of the rhyme-prose, these *yüeh-fu* songs (so-called because of their source) from the Han were a continuation, both in terms of content and structure, of the tradition of the *Shih-ching*, especially of the lyric convention in the *Feng* section. These poems also illustrated the development of the new poetic form. The growing popularity of the pentasyllabic verse had already been found in a few court songs in the Martial Emperor's reign, such as the lyric song attributed to the court musician Li Yen-nien ("In the north there is a beautiful lady") (I, 102). Most of the *yüeh-fu* songs attributed to the later Eastern Han period adopted the form. These not only exceeded the earlier fragmentary folk rhymes in length, but also in their richer contents and more refined diction. Probably because of their close relation with the accompanying music, these songs were widely circulated, and were soon to find a response in the writings of the literati.

During the evolution of the basic prosodic form (from tetrasyllabic to pentasyllabic verse), the stanzaic structure as found in the *Shih-ching* also gave up its predominant place to the linear structure, but the basic structural pattern of starting with scenic description and closing with statement of sentiment or thought continued, as shown in the following example, one of the *Longer Songs* (*Ch'ang ko hsing*):

> Green, green, the hollyhocks in the garden,
> The morning dew on them will disappear in the sun.
> Warm spring bestows its generous grace around,
> Everything in the world shines in its light.
> Often one fears the approaching autumn
> When flowers and leaves turn yellow and wither;
> Hundreds of rivers flow east, towards the sea:
> When will they ever return west?
> If no effort is ever made in youth,
> Then in old age only sorrow remains! (I, 262)

The poem starts with an image, that of the hollyhock plants in the garden covered by morning dew. It is spring, and everything is fresh and bright. Yet, probably from the thought that the dew may dry up in the sunshine when noon approaches, the singer's mood suddenly turns to anguish in the middle of the poem. He starts deploring the coming autumn season, when the scene of light and luxuriance in front of his eyes will be replaced by one of desolation and decay. This is superseded by a metaphor of the rivers, a symbol of the fleeting time. Now the speaker's thoughts are directed to the human cycle. The closing couplet brings out the *carpe diem* theme of the song: one should not waste time in youth. Though different in prosodic form, its basic structural order, typical of the *yüeh-fu* poems in general, is remarkably similar to that of the lyric songs in the *Feng* section of the *Shih-ching*.

In a few *yüeh-fu* poems, however, we could trace certain subtle changes in the use of images and the shifting of their positions. We may have a look, for example, at the poem entitled *Song of Flying Swans* (*Fei hu hsing*). Like a typical *Shih-ching* song, it starts with a beginning in affective image:

> There came flying pairs of white swans
> Which had come from the northwest.

Instead of switching to a statement of the occasion or event and presenting the theme of the poem, usually after the first two lines as the *Shih-ching* texts so often do, this poem continues the image of these white swans, making them the main figures of the poem. It goes on to tell how one of these swans suddenly becomes sick and is unable to catch up with its mate and the company, and how its mate looks back and flies around again and again, distressed by the separation. The poem even assumes the voice of that swan (ll. 9–16):

> I want to hold you in my bills and take you away,
> Silent with fear, I cannot open my bills;
> I want to carry you away on my back,
> Yet my plumage is wearing away, day by day.
> It's pleasant to make new acquaintance,
> But it's sad to part, and never to meet again.
> Faltering, I look back on the other company,
> Tears trickle down, crisscrossing my face.

As we have discussed in the previous chapter, the opening image in the *Shih-ching* poems is frequently used to evoke associations. But a *yüeh-fu* poem like this one devotes the main body of the text to amplifying that image, making the entire poem into an allegory of associations. However, the poem then closes with a couplet entirely irrelevant to the image, obviously a continuation of the conventional entertainer's closure in words of blessing (ll. 17–18):

> This day we enjoy having fun together,
> May you live on for ten thousand years. (I, 272)[5]

In some *yüeh-fu* songs, like the following *Song of Sorrow* (*Pei ko*), the mode of *pi* (trope) is used at the end:

> A sad song may take the place of weeping,
> Looking afar: a substitute for home-going.

When I think about my native place,
My heart becomes gloomy and weary.
I want to go back: no one left at home.
I want to cross the river, but have no boat.
I cannot put my thoughts in words,
Within my intestines, wheels turn around. (I, 282)

The last line here adopts a metaphor which may sound weird to an English reader, who need to know that the Chinese term *ch'ang* or "intestines" is often used figuratively in a sense not unlike the English word *heart*. The closure presents a powerful image that has since become a conventional metaphor for anguish or anxiety.[6] The connection between the image of wheels revolving and that of the intestines (presumably coiling in pain) is one of association. It is interesting to notice that the closing image comes after a penultimate line about the speaker's frustration with the limitation of language. It is generally at a moment of silence that an image is to display its most appealing effect.

The group of poems known as the *Nineteen Old Poems* (*Ku-shih shih-chiu-shou*) was probably composed in the second half of the second century, when the Eastern Han was hastening to its final collapse. These poems, probably literati reworking of earlier *yüeh-fu* texts, firmly established the pentasyllabic verse as the dominant Chinese poetic form, and marked the highest achievement of Chinese lyric poetry since the *Shih-ching*. They not only carried on the conventions of *fu, pi* and *hsing* in the ancient model, but also further enriched them by shifting their positions or making them more complex in structure. One of these conventions is the use of scenic beginning, which may bear direct description (*fu*) of the scene or setting of the poem, or carry a strong sense of figurative (*pi*) or affective / associative (*hsing*) function, such as in the following examples:

(No. 2)
Green, green, grass on riverbank;
Lush, lush, willow in the garden.
Pretty, pretty, the lady up in the tower—
Bright, bright, she sits right at the window. (I, 329)

(No. 5)
To the northwest stands a tall tower
That levels with floating clouds in height:
Lattice windows, fine silk screens,
Curved eaves above three stories of steps. (I, 330)

(No. 7)
The clear moon shines, bright at night,
The cricket chirps by the eastern wall.
The Jade Bar signals the coming of winter,
Clusters of stars, how splendid they are! (I, 330)

(No. 11)
The eastern city walls are tall and long,
Far and wide they turn and stretch.
A whirling wind rises, shaking the ground,
Gone is the green of the autumn grass. (I, 332)

Some of the poems in this group, as the following examples may illustrate, bear much resemblance to the *Shih-ching* poems that employ the mode of *hsing* at the beginning, in that no overt connection exists between the starting image and the subsequent thought:

(No. 3)
Green, green, cypress on the hills,
Heaps on heaps, stones in the creek.
Man, living between earth and heaven,
Hurries on, like a wayfarer in distant land. (I, 329)

(No. 8)
Frail, frail, bamboos growing in the wild,
Their roots clasp to the mountain's edge.
Newly wed to you, my sire,
A creeper clings to the moss. (I, 331)

The closure of these poems, on the other hand, are mostly statements of sentiment or thought. Many of the poems close in lament, in agreement with the pervading melancholy that characterizes the entire group:

(No. 6)
Sharing one heart, but living apart,
Sadly goes our life, till old age and end. (I, 330)

(No. 16)
Walk around or stand still, sad in heart,
I shed tears on the two door leaves. (I, 333)

(No. 19)
Going outside the doors, I rambled alone.

Who's there to tell my sad thoughts to?
I turned back into the chamber again,
My tears trickled down, damping my clothes. (I, 334)

In a few of them the closure provides a kind of philosophical, reflective conclusion: ironical, frequently bitter, realization of the hard truth of life and society:

(No. 1)
Let it be, and say no further!
Just make some effort to eat more. (I, 329)

(No. 4)
Why don't you whip your tall horse,
Get ahead of others and grab key positions?
Why should you stay poor and humble,
And tumble along in constant distress! (I, 330)

(No. 11)
Human life is not metal or rock,
How can it last for very long?
Swiftly it passes away with things,
A name of glory, that is the prize! (I, 332)

In all the above examples, the closure follows the dominant pattern of the *Shih-ching* texts, and exerts a strong concluding effect. The two poems as follows, however, differ from the rest of the group in their use of figurative language at the ending:

(No. 5)
Let us become a pair of cranes that, crying,
Flutter wings and soar high aloft! (I, 330)

(No. 12)
If only we could be a pair of flying swallows
That carry clay to nest under your eaves. (I, 332)

It has been noted that this type of ending derived from the closure of one of the songs in the *Shih-ching*:

I mused upon it in the quiet
And wished I could fly up and away![7]

But, compared to its antecedent, the closure of these two texts from the *Nineteen Old Poems* is more visual. It is in fact an integration of two closing patterns in the *Shih-ching*: the wishful closure and the simile closure. The former usually suggests something in sharp contrast to what is described in the poem (*here* and *now*)—something that lies beyond the real world of the speaker (*then* and *there*). In the *Shih-ching* texts that adopt such a type of closure, it is usually an abstract or factual statement of desire. With the *Nineteen Old Poems*, the desire is sometimes complemented and enhanced by the vivid pictorial image of the closing simile. A similar combination was also found in a few of the *yüeh-fu* songs of the time, which suggests to us that it might have been a common practice of the age. The associations of the images had already been developed in the *yüeh-fu* tradition, but the anonymous author(s) of the *Old Poems* seemed to have begun to move such images to the end, embedding them within an explicit statement of wish or desire.

During and after the Chien-an period (196–219), renowned for its achievement in literature (especially in poetry), the pentasyllabic verse was widely adopted and further perfected by various poets, but the *Nineteen Old Poems*, along with the group of poems conventionally though falsely attributed to Su Wu and Li Ling, and a few *yüeh-fu* songs as well, remained the paradigm and *beau ideal* of the form, duplicated and imitated by all major poets. The basic structural pattern of starting with image and closing with thought was continued with little variation. This was found in the poetry of most leading poets from the Wei to the Chin dynasties, including the three Ts'ao (father and sons), Juan Chi, Hsi K'ang, Lu Chi, and P'an Yüeh. The statement of feeling at the end of the poem was further developed and strengthened in their works. However, in the works of two poets from this period (generally known as the Six Dynasties), Tso Ssu and T'ao Ch'ien, a subtle transition of the closure patterns was reflected.

Among the poets of the Western Chin dynasty (265-316), the poetry of Tso Ssu demonstrated a kind of *other-ness* in contrast to most of its author's predecessors and contemporaries. Scanty as his extant poems are (some fourteen of them altogether), they seem to display a particular concern with closure. His *Poems on Historical Themes* (*Yung-shih shih*), a sequence of eight poems, expressed his own aspirations and his indignation at social injustice, through the discussion of a number of historical figures. The first poem of the sequence is a kind of self-portrait that serves as a prefatory piece to the series:

At twenty, I played with the soft writing brush,
Lofty-minded, I perused books of all kinds.
In expository essay, I modelled on *Reproving Ch'in*,
For descriptive rhyme-prose, I emulated *Master Imaginary*.
When frontier towns came beleaguered under whizzing arrows,
When clarion call took wings all the way from the capital,
Though not a warrior wearing armor and helmet,
I became well-versed in Jang-chü's *Art of War*.
I shouted loud and long, my voice rending the air,
In my mind the Eastern Wu had already been wiped out.[8]
Even a blunt knife would have its moment for one cut,
So I dreamed about how my ambitions would all come true:
To the east, I'd clear the Yangtze and Hsiang rivers;
To the west, I'd subdue the barbaric Ch'iang and Hu.
Once the task be done, I'd decline all honor and rank,
Make a deep bow, and return to my country home. (I, 732)

The poem starts with an account of the speaker's literary and military preoccupations in youth, moves on to tell us about his aspirations to win glory and honor for the nation, and concludes with a description of his noble dream. The two closing lines contain an allusion to a historical figure of the Warring States period, Lu Chung-lien of the state of Ch'i, who declined all the rank and wealth awarded him for his peace-making accomplishment, and went into seclusion afterwards. The closure presents a structured gesture that epitomizes the self-portrait. Almost all the other poems in Tso Ssu's poetic sequence have endings that carry a sense of emphatic conclusion. This was frequently achieved by the use of rhetorical question, and of *litotes* (italicized in text) that intensifies the force of the speaker's emotions:

(No. 2)
Master Feng, was he *not* a man of great talent?[9]
Hoary with age, still *not* summoned for office! (I, 733)

(No. 7)
What age did *not* have extraordinary talents
To be left and forgot in the wilderness! (I, 734)

In particular, the closure of the fifth poem in the sequence presents another symbolic gesture like that of the first poem. It is further enriched by being structured within a sublime scenic background:

I'd shake dust from my clothes on cliff a thousand *jen* tall,

And bathe my feet in the river that flows for ten thousand *li*.[10] (I, 733)

Admittedly such closure in a gesture, as found in the first and the fifth poems of Tso Ssu's sequence, is still less a visualized image than a conceptualized ideal. It displays, as the other endings of Tso Ssu's poems do, an attention to the rich potential of poetic closure not found in his contemporaries as well as his predecessors.

Like Tso Ssu, T'ao Ch'ien was not in the literary mainstream of his own time, and was underestimated by his contemporaries and immediate successors. His poetic talent, probably going ahead of his own age, was not fully recognized until the High T'ang. Unlike the emotional lines of Tso Ssu, though, T'ao Ch'ien's poetry tends to be more controlled in emotion, and there is always an unhurried tempo throughout the text. Neither the surprise beginning of Ts'ao Chih nor the forceful ending of Tso Ssu is to be found in his poems. The majority of his poems close in the traditional format of thought or sentiment. But, under the influence of the growing metaphysical concern of his age, and in the convention of the *Nineteen Old Poems*, T'ao Ch'ien frequently chose to add a philosophical touch at the end:

(*Back to My Farmhouse: Five Poems*, No. 5)
Human life is like an illusion
That returns eventually to nothingness. (II, 992)

(*Drinking Wine: Twenty Poems*, No. 8)
Our life is within dream and illusion:
What's our purpose to stay in earthly bonds? (II, 999)

(*A Poem Blaming My Sons*)
Since this is my lot, as Heaven so wills,
I'll just have more of what's in my glass. (II, 1002–1003)

A remarkable thing about the patterns of T'ao Ch'ien's poetic closure is that the conventional statement of thought is often combined with or framed within an image, as in the following examples:

(*Matching Poems by Assistant Magistrate Kuo*, No. 1)
Watching the white clouds, far and wide,
How deeply I long for ancient times! (II, 978)

(*Valediction to A Friend at General Wang's Party*)
Seeing off the returning boat far in the distance,

I leave my feelings to Nature's myriad changes. (II, 981)

(*Drinking Wine: Twenty Pieces*, No. 5)
The mountain air is nice at sunset,
Birds fly together on their way back;
Inside all this there is a truth,
I want to find it, but forget the words. (II, 998)

(Ibid., No. 7)
The sun sets, all moving things are at rest,
Home-going birds honk on their way to the woods;
I proudly whistle by the eastern window:
I have lived another day of this life. (II, 998)

In all these examples, the last line or couplet that makes a statement of the poet's feelings is preceded by a penultimate line or couplet that presents an image. In the first two examples, within the frame of the scene there is a structured gesture of the poet as spectator. In the next two examples the image is no longer a mere object (*wu*) as found in most of the *Shih-ching* poems, but a larger landscape or scene of Nature. Although the image was not yet moved all the way to the end, it was nevertheless approaching that position; it also became more sophisticated than those in the ancient models in that it was closely woven into a texture of emotions.

It was only during the Liang Dynasty at the beginning of the sixth century, when poetry received the patronage from members of the imperial house, that signs of basic change in poetic closure emerged. Breaking with the tradition of closing with sentiment or thought, the Liang court poets sometimes chose to have pure scenic description throughout the text. As an example, consider one of the nature poems by the leader of the "court poets" Hsiao Kang, the crowned prince who later reigned as Emperor Chien-wen for a brief period of two years that ended in his assassination:

Written on the day of Wu Yin, the Tenth Month, the Year 544)

Noise and dust, by now, have settled down;
Quietly I sit facing layers of mountains:
Winter is deep, willow twigs have fallen;
Snow has deprived cassias of their flowers.
Stars are bright, mist is cleared away;
The sky is white, swans march in single lines.
Soaring clouds, at times, resemble towers;

Frozen ices, from far away, seem like silk.
Late-grown oranges hide behind folds of screens,
Withered vines cling to twisting poles.
Shady reeds border on the steam of waterside,
Mountain peaks adds to the chill of the moon. (III, 1948)

Everything here is observed as if through a painter's eye. Every line of the poem is composed like from a stroke of the landscape painter's brush. In terms of its structure, this poem is characteristic of most descriptive court poems of the age. Here, as in some other poems by Emperor Chien-wen and his courtiers, the final couplet also consists of images. But since the overall structure is one of paratactic enumeration of descriptions, the closure is a mere continuation of that pattern. In such poems, it always seems as if the poet could either move on further, or just end here because he had run out of descriptions. Although the poem ends without a sense of conclusion, there was yet no dynamic shift preceding the scenic closure as exemplified in some of Tu Fu's poems. Nor was there anything in the sense of Tu Fu's "further space" or "the vast" beyond these endings, as advocated by the T'ang master. Still such closure was an obvious deviation from the standard pattern of closing with expression of thought: the poet found it sufficient to talk about what he observed, and was under no compulsion to add a statement of his mind or of his reaction to the scene.

Literary change and evolution do not necessarily synchronize with the arbitrary periodization of dynastic history. The T'ang empire, established in the year of 618, swiftly rose to its prime of political stability and economic prosperity during the Chen-kuan reign (627–649). Yet, in the realm of poetry and literature, the first six to seven decades of the new dynasty saw primarily a continuation of the conventions of the late Southern Dynasties in terms of style, diction, structure and themes. It was not until the beginning of the eighth century that signs of poetic innovation emerged, and an increasingly stronger new voice began to make itself heard. However, one has to bear in mind that the development of poetry is largely a gradual process, and literary changes frequently cannot be brought about in a matter of a few years, or even a few decades. A careful examination of poetic structure, of the ways poem end, will help to reconstruct a picture of one aspect of this gradual movement.

Few critics, for example, have attributed any innovative talent to Yü Shih-nan, who served in both the Sui and the T'ang court. The thirty odd poems that make up his surviving poetic *oeuvre* are restricted to *yüeh-fu* style songs or court poems of assigned topics— mostly "poems on objects" (*yung-wu shih*). One of his poems in the first type, entitled *Going Beyond the Frontiers* (*Ch'u sai*), describes an aging military general on an expedition beyond the frontier (north of the Great Wall). The poem starts discursively, but moves on to a description of the desolate scene of snowy mountains and frozen rivers. Its semantic structure reverses the normal pattern of image first and thought afterward. The poem closes with an image of the general standing alone in the darkening twilight:

> Upright and worthy, he leaned on his long sword.
> The sun's setting, it darkened, amid wind and dust.[11]

The closing image here contains a gesture of the aging general. The gesture is framed in a scene that calls forth in the reader's mind the dangerous situation of fighting in unknown land. The setting sun and the darkening twilight are associated with the general's age. This closure was an unusual one in early T'ang poetry, and its symbolic image seemed to be a precursor of the closure of Tu Fu's *Beautiful Lady*.

Similar examples of scenic closure began to appear in *yüeh-fu* style songs by various poets of the second half of the seventh century. Let us look at a few examples from that period:

Lu Chao-ling: *Ch'ang-an: An Old Theme*

> Of yore, here stood white-jade hall with golden steps.
> By now, only green pine-trees appear in sight.
> Lonely and dreary, at Master Yang's old lodge,[12]
> Year in, year out, just lies a couch heaped with books,
> Only the cassia trees in southern hills are in flower,
> Their petals fly here and there, attaching to clothes. (II, 518–519)

Li Ch'iao: *Song of Fen-yin*

> Don't you see now, over the river of Fen,
> Year after year, only the autumn geese fly? (III, 689–690)

Wang Po: *Atop a Tall Tower*

> Just watch where the tall towers stood in days bygone,
> At Cypress Beam and Bronze Bird,[13] only yellow dust stirs. (III, 672)

Tower of Prince T'eng[14]

The royal son in the tower—now where is he?
Outside the gate, only the Yangtze flows by itself. (III, 673)

Liu Hsi-yi: In the Tune of *Lament for the Hoary Old Man*

Just watch places where they sang and danced in the past,
Now, at dusk, there is nothing but birds flying around. (III, 885–886)

Most of these poems close with reference to the theme of life's brevity and the precariousness of prosperity and power, through a sharp contrast between the glory of a place in the past and the desolate scene at present. Instead of making a discursive comment on or an explicit response to such a change, the speakers in these poems choose to use imperatives or questions, inviting their audience to observe the scene, and leaving it to their own interpretation or judgment. The rhetorical question "Don't you see" (*chün pu chien*) came to be widely used at the ending through the next few generations, especially in poems in conventional *yüeh-fu* or pseudo-*yüeh-fu* forms. Notably, in all these examples, the scenic closure develops around the motif of the absence of human beings. The subjectivity of the speaker lies hidden behind an invitation to the reader to watch an "objective" scene.

It was such endings, carrying within them a strong sense of invitation or appeal, that led to the practice of the major poets of the eighth century who, as Stephen Owen has pointed out, developed new forms of poetic endings, such as the ones using images designed to stir a response in the reader.[15] As I have argued in the previous chapter, this development was made through a shifting of the position of the affective image (*hsing*) to the end of a poem.

The High T'ang saw a constellation of major poets, of which Tu Fu was one of the brightest stars.[16] Although Tu Fu used the scenic closure with great skill, he should not be considered its inventor, nor its sole practitioner. The use of scenic closure is found in the works of a few of his seniors as well as in those of his many contemporaries. The image was still embedded in explicit statement of wish or feeling in the *yüeh-fu* and *ku-shih* conventions. But the supporting frame of mental activity was sometimes removed, leaving only the image to speak for itself; and the image was often impregnated with rich emotions. One example of such a closure is found in a pentasyllabic regulated octave by Meng Hao-jan:

Returning to Southern Mountains at the Year's End

Submit no more memorial to the imperial Northern Archway,
Return to my shabby lodge at the Southern Mountains.
A man of no talent, I've been forsaken by our sage ruler,
Delicate in health, I now shy away from old acquaintances.
White hairs grow, hastening my life to old age;
Spring greenness is soon to overtake the year's end.
Harboring a long sorrow in mind, I am sleepless:
Pines, the moon, the night, the window—empty. (V, 1651–1652)

If we place this poem side by side with a lyric song from the *Shih-ching* or with one of the *Nineteen Old Poems*, the contrast becomes remarkable: the structure of this poem reverses the old pattern. Instead of starting with images and going on to an explicit statement of thought or feeling, as found in the early models, Meng Hao-jan's poem does just the opposite. It devotes all but the last line of the poem to a discursive reflection, which yields to a purely descriptive scene only at the end. The penultimate line of the poem would make a typical conclusion in earlier poetry, as frequently seen in Juan Chi's *Yung-huai* (*Telling My Thoughts*) poems. The last line, which consists of a set of images, would be less unusual had it appeared in any of the middle lines of any other contemporary poem. It is its very position in the text that endows the poem with the so-called "voice of the High T'ang" (*sheng T'ang chih yin*). The closure names a group of things in an essentially indeterminate or undefined relation. While the first four words (*Pines, the moon, the night, the window*) in the last line bespeak concrete images, the last word (*empty*) is both descriptive and emotional.

The following frequently anthologized poem by Wang Wei is another fine example of the use of scenic closure:

In Reply to District Defender Chang

In my late years I only enjoy tranquility,
The myriad of worldly things are not my concern.
On self-reflection: I have no long-term plans;
All I know is to return to my old woods.
Winds blow through the pines, loosening my girdle,
Moon over mountains shines on me, while I play the zither.
You ask about the pattern of life's ups and downs?
A fisherman's song fades deep into the river mouth. (IV, 1267)

Like the previous text, this poem is also in the form of a pentasyllabic regulated octave, which usually keeps a quadripartite structure, with each of its four couplets playing a different function. In this poem, the structure also reverses the traditional pattern of starting with image and turning on to ideas. The opening couplet is a statement of thought: it tells the speaker's present state of mind. An underlying tension is felt beneath the calm surface. As has been suggested, if the poet "only enjoy(s) tranquility" in his *late* years, then how about his *early* and his *middle* years?[17] Was he more engaged in activity (the contrary to *tranquility*) in the past? If so, what accounted for his change at present? If nothing in the world concerns him *now*, did he concern himself with things *then*? The expression *late years* thus sets up a temporal point that provides room for contrast, and builds up the inherent tension of the text.

The second couplet, following the conventional structure, is a continuation of the first. It tells us about his present state of mind, and the tension found in the preceding couplet continues. If he had no *long-term plans* now, did he ever have any? If so, what made him give them up? What is there in the *old woods* that appeals to him?

It is not until the third couplet that the poem makes a switch, as the *neck couplet* usually does as structurally designated, and presents a picture of the poet himself sitting in the moonlight, presumably back in his *old woods*. The loosening of the girdle indicates a gesture of intimacy, an embrace of Nature itself as represented by the wind in the pines and the moon over the mountains. By Wang Wei's age, the image of a Chinese poet playing the zither always carried in it the connotation of the yearning for "one who understands the sound" (*chih-yin*), as the ancient musician Po Ya found in his friend Chung Tzu-ch'i.[18]

The last couplet harks back to the title: the poem was written as a reply to a poem from District Defender Chang. The penultimate line refers to a question that Chang presumably raised in his poem to Wang Wei. Instead of giving an answer to the question, the poet offers in the last line offers a kind of auditory image (*fisherman's song*) that evokes an visual image as well. The reader may imagine a landscape: at the mouth of a river hidden by high reeds, the fisherman is no longer to be seen, but the sound of his singing can still be heard. Apparently, the line does not respond to the question, or does it? How is this image related to the preceding question? What kind of connection is there between the pattern of life's vicissitudes and a fisherman's song? It almost sounds like a Ch'an (Zen) Buddhist puzzle (*gatha*) that Wang Wei must have acquainted himself with through his admiration for the great Ch'an master Hui-neng.[19]

However, any educated reader of Wang Wei's time would recognize in the ending the important intertext of *The Fisherman* (*Yü-fu*), a short prose piece in the *Ch'u-tz'u* collection which consists of an imaginary dialogue. During his exile Ch'ü Yüan ran into an anonymous fisherman, and they started a debate on whether one should hold an active or a passive attitude towards society. Ch'ü Yüan maintained his Confucian principle of uncompromising righteousness; the fisherman advocated the different values of "riding the tide of the times", i.e., serving the state only when it would be fruitful, and withdrawing from the world when it would not. Seeing that he could not persuade Ch'ü Yüan, the fisherman rowed away singing:

> When the waters of the Blue Waves are clear,
> I can wash my hat ribbons in them;
> When the waters of the Blue Waves are turbid,
> I can wash my feet in them.[20]

This intertext provides the clue to the philosophical message that Wang Wei was trying to pass on to his reader. The expression *fisherman's song* in the last line is the key phrase that calls forth the allusion, and gives the entire text a political perspective. The poem can be deceptive: the peaceful and calm tone almost dominates it until the last couplet, and even then the message is an implicit one. A little exploration into Wang Wei's biographical background may shed further light on our interpretation of this poem, We know that from 739 to 755, Wang Wei enjoyed imperial favor, and served in a relatively high court position; but he seemed to enjoy in his privacy much more than in carrying out his official responsibilities. He sought, and perhaps really found, peace and comfort at his Wang-ch'uan Villa, which he acquired in 747, in the scenic, mountainous suburbs of the capital Ch'ang-an. Most of the poems that he wrote at the estate seemed to be quietly, almost imperturbably, bucolic. In creating such an illusionary world, Wang Wei was under the influence of his favorite precursor T'ao Ch'ien, who once wrote these lines (*Drinking Wine: Twenty Poems*, No. 5):

> My lodge was built well within the human world,
> Yet I hear not noise of chaises and horses;

One may ask: how could you have achieved that?
My mind is far away, so the place becomes remote. (II, 998)

During this period, the talented and conscientious Chang Chiu-ling, a friend of Wang Wei's, was dismissed from his post as prime minister. He was replaced by Li Lin-fu, a notorious politician known as "honey-mouthed and dagger-hearted" (*k'ou mi fu chien*) who earned the disapproval and hostility of most civil officials for his manipulation of court politics. Wang Wei, with his prestigious and powerful aristocratic family background, continued to be treated well in Li Lin-fu's administration. It was therefore interesting to notice that in his Wang-ch'uan poems, Wang Wei frequently turned to echoing the poetry of Tao Ch'ien, who literally forsook all his official positions.

While the Confucian ideal always directed a Chinese intellectual like Wang Wei to keep serving the state, the apolitical Taoism and Buddhism would help him to find relief and refuge in retreat. Perhaps ill at ease in the tense factionalism of court politics, Wang Wei seemed to have chosen to keep his mind *far away*, to resort to a refuge of his own, and to stay as close as possible to nature.

The closure of the poem suggests a choice. Around that choice, though, there is much tension. In the source text of *The Fisherman*, there is a strong contrast between Ch'ü Yüan's Confucian idea of social responsibility and personal integrity, and the fisherman's Taoist concept of flexibility. The story about Ch'ü Yüan's eventual drowning in the Hsiang River has demonstrated that the exiled Ch'u statesman and poet had eventually made his choice: an uncompromising suicide rather than "wallowing in the mire" of dirty politics. By thus restructuring the *Ch'u-tz'u* text into his poem, Wang Wei seemed to have placed his emphasis on the difficulty of choice, though the contrast after the transposition is perhaps just as strong. On the one hand, Wang Wei could not help but notice the corruption and treachery of court politics, and it was painful and morally degenerating to him that he still had to serve, unable to do anything to improve the situation. On the other hand, he seemed to hope, or tried to make himself believe, that by retreating to his villa and getting close to nature, he could somehow retain his personal integrity. All the tension, all the conflicts in mind, of which the poet makes no explicit statement in the poem, are revealed through the equivocal, enigmatic last image at its end.

In comparison to the rich allusions of Wang Wei's poem, the

following poem, a pentasyllabic quatrain by Li Po, seems to have a much less complex texture:

Lament at the Jade Doorsteps

At the jade doorsteps, white dew grew;
Night was long, it crept into gauze socks.
But then she pulled down the crystal curtain
To watch through it the dainty autumn moon. (V, 1701)

Except for the word *Lament* (*yüan*) in the title, there is not a single word referring to human emotions throughout the entire text. The poem is basically about an enclosed world: a courtyard within the walls of the imperial palace, and at its middle the boudoir of a court lady. The description of this enclosed world is nevertheless constantly remindful of the open world outside: through the dew, the moon, and the autumn season that link up both worlds. Whiteness is the dominant color through the text: the white dew, the jade (white and smooth) doorsteps, the autumn moon, and the whiteness of the female body only remotely suggested within the synecdochic *gauze socks*. The court lady, unseen in entirety, makes herself felt throughout the text. She was the one who stayed through the long night outside at the doorsteps, so long, that the night dew infiltrated her gauze socks. She was the one who pulled down the crystal curtain. Did she do that to keep the moist outside? or to prepare to go to bed? She was the one who, even after getting inside her chamber, still watched the moon, which she might have already watched for a long time while she stayed outside, instead of going to sleep. The season of the year, spelled out not until in the last line, is the conventional season of melancholy.[21] Each of the twenty words in the original text passes some information or hidden message to the reader. The poem speaks through fragments which, when placed together, compose a unified image.

Short as it is, the poem is presented in a linear structure that speaks of a duration, of a series of movements. In the first half, the subject of the two predicates, *grew* (*sheng*) and *crept* (*ch'in*), bespeaks of Nature (as represented by the dew). In the latter half, the two predicates, *pulled down* (*hsia*) and *watch* (*wang*), refer to the human figure in the scene. Just as part of her body is covered within the thin gauze stockings, the hidden message of sorrow in her heart (made explicit only by the word *Lament* in the title) is under the disguise of the apparent transparency of the text as provided by the expression *crystal curtain*, a meta-poetic metaphor as I see it. Both are deceptive barriers that the reader has to see through on his own.

Between the title and the text there brews a tension that invites the reader to find clues for the puzzle. The last line, apparently purely descriptive, prompts a series of questions. Why did the lady stay awake for such a long time in an autumn night? Why did she keep watching the moon even after getting inside? What does the moon stand for in the culture and what kind of emotions or things does it evoke in one's mind? Exactly because the poem ends the ways it does, in a visual image apparently devoid of any emotional message, it opens up room for further meditations on its layers and layers of meaning between the lines.

From a few examples above, we can see how the High T'ang masters adopted the scenic closure in their poems, and used it in as varied and rich ways as found in Tu Fu's poetry. In fact the scenic closure was firmly established as a structural device by the age, and was continued through later poetic tradition. In particular, the scenic closure was extensively used in the lyric songs (*tz'u*), the new poetic form that came of its age in the last years of the T'ang dynasty and flourished in the Sung dynasty. Was the adoption of the scenic closure recognized by the critics as well as the poets themselves as a conscious, innovative poetic device? What was the philosophical and aesthetic foundation of the scenic closure, leaving the images to speak for themselves? What was the relation between the poet's conscious effort in his practice, and the reader's awareness in the reading process? These are some of the questions to be examined in the next chapter. An exploration of these questions will help to illuminate some of the fundamental features of Chinese poetry.

Notes

1. Hsiao T'ung comp., *P'ing-chu Chao-ming Wen-hsüan*, ed. by Yü Kuang-hua (1778, reprint., Taipei: Hsüeh-hai ch'u-pan-she, 1981), p. 95. Ch'eng (reigned 1104–1068 B.C.) and K'ang (reigned 1067–1042 B.C.) were kings of early Western Chou dynasty, when the hymns in the *Sung* section of the *Shih-ching* were supposed to have been composed. For an English translation of Pan Ku's work, with extensive critical notes, see David R. Knechtges translated, with Annotations and Introduction, *Wen Xuan or Selections of Refined Literature*, Vol. I: *Rhapsodies on Metropolises and Capitals*

(Princeton: Princeton University Press, 1982): pp. 72–179.

2. The *Ch'u-tz'u* (*The Songs of the South*), an anthology compiled by Wang Yi, an imperial librarian in the second century A. D., consists mainly of texts dated to late fourth century and third century B.C., attributed to Ch'ü Yüan, an aristocrat of the southern state of Ch'u, and some of his immediate successors. It should be noted here that the literary form represented by those texts attributed to Ch'ü Yüan in the anthology, which came to the central stage of Chinese literature in the third century B.C., has frequently been considered in the Chinese critical tradition as belonging to an independent genre called the *sao*, from the title of *Li-sao* (*Encountering Sorrow*), as different from the *shih* poetry as represented by the *Shih-ching* texts. In *Wen-hsin tiao-lung*, for example, Liu Hsieh discussed the two forms respectively in the chapters of "An Analysis of *Sao*" (*Pien sao*) and "An Exegesis of *Shih*" (*Ming shih*). The *Ch'u-tz'u* certainly has exerted a great perennial influence on the later development of Chinese *shih* poetry, but the texts in the collection, being mostly the products of a region where at that historical moment local Ch'u culture of the Yangtze River area prospered side by side with the northern culture of the Yellow River area (as Professor Kwang-chih Chang has convincingly verified in his archaeological studies), are not only much longer in length than most lyric songs in the *Shih-ching*, but also assume very different prosodic forms. The subtle but important relation between the *Shih-ching* and the *Ch'u-tz'u*, however, is beyond the range of our discussion here. The *Ch'u-tz'u* has found an excellent English translation. See *The Songs of the South: An Ancient Anthology of Poems by Qu Yuan and Other Poets*, translated, annotated, and introduced by David Hawkes (Harmondsworth, Middlesex: Penguin Books, 1985). See also Kwang-chih Chang, *The Archaeology of Ancient China* (New Haven, Connecticut: Yale University Press, rev. ed., 1969), 408.

3. See *Liang Han wen-hsüeh-shih ts'an-k'ao tzu-liao*, ed. by the Teaching and Research Group of the History of Chinese Literature, Peking University (Peking: Chung-hua shu-chü, 1962), pp. 561–63.

4. See Lu Ch'in-li ed. *Hsien-Ch'in Han Wei Chin nan-pei-ch'ao shih* (Peking: Chung-hua shu-chü, 3 Vols., 1983), I, pp. 255–297. I have not included in my count here the fragmentary couplets included in the two *chüan* of *yüeh-fu* songs in the anthology. All further citations of pre-T'ang poems, unless specifically noted, are from this anthology, with the volume number and pagination given parenthetically in the text.

5. A slightly varied text forms the first part, or a prelude, for another song bearing the same title (in some versions *White Cranes*) (273), which is complemented by lines assuming the voice of a human couple. The form of closure in words of blessing is shared by both texts, and with some slight variations of wording, also found in a few other *yüeh-fu* songs of the period, e.g., *Song of the White-headed* (274), *Song in Slow Rhythm* (282), and the two poems both entitled *Old Song* (289, 295).

6. The beautiful *yüeh-fu* song *Old Song* (289) has the same ending. It is frequently used as a closing image in the later *ku-shih* ("old [style] poems") convention.

7. This is the ending of *Po-chou* (No. 26) in the *Feng* section of the *Shih-ching*. For an observation on the similarity of the closures see Ma Mao-yüan, *Ku-shih shih-chiu-shou t'an-so* (Peking: Tso-chia ch'u-pan-she, 1957), p. 81.

8. *Reproving the Ch'in* was a famous essay written by the Han writer Chia Yi (201–169 B.C.). *Master Imaginary* was written by the eminent Han rhyme-prose writer Ssu-ma Hsiang-ju (179–117 B.C.). Ssu-ma Jang-chü was the defense minister of the Ch'i

dukedom during the reign of Duke Ching (547–490 B.C.). His comments on the art of war was edited at the authorization of King Wei-wang of the Ch'i kingdom (reigned 356–320 B.C.). The state of the Eastern Wu was eliminated in the year of 280.

9. Master Feng was Feng T'ang, who was a courtier under the reign of Emperor Wen-ti (180–157 B.C.) of the Han dynasty. He was said to be a talented man who did not get any appointment until he was very old.

10. Chinese measurements vary according to place and age. A *jen* is approximately 98.7 inches, or a little more than 8 feet, and a *li* is roughly one third of a mile.

11. *Ch'üan T'ang shih* (Shanghai: Chung-hua shu-chü, 25 Vols., 1985), II, p. 471. All subsequent citations from T'ang poems are from this version, with the volume number and pagination given parenthetically in the text. This poem was also attributed to Yü Shih-nan's elder brother Yü Shih-chi (d. 618), whose works were included in collections of pre-T'ang poetry. See Lu Ch'in-li, III, p. 2710.

12. Master Yang was Yang Hsiung (53 B.C.–A.D. 18), a Han philosopher and writer known for his erudition.

13. Cypress Beam Terrace (*Po-liang t'ai*), located inside the northern gate of the city of Ch'ang-an, was constructed by order of the Martial Emperor of the Han dynasty in the spring of 115 B.C. According to an interesting anecdote in *Description of the Three Capitals* (*San-fu huang-t'u*), a sixth-century guidebook to the capital of Ch'ang-an, the Martial Emperor often held banquets for his courtiers at the terrace, and only those who could compose heptasyllabic lines were invited to join and composed linked verse. The kind of heptasyllabic linked verse was later known as the "Cypress Beam style." Bronze Bird Terrace (*T'ung-ch'üeh t'ai*) was constructed at the order of the poet and statesman Ts'ao Ts'ao (155–220) in 210.

14. Tower of Prince T'eng, a riverside building in Kiangsi province, was constructed in 659 by the order of Li Yüan-ying (Prince T'eng), then Prefect of Hung-chou. Wang Po wrote a famous rhyme-prose preface to his poem on the tower.

15. Owen, *The Poetry of the Early T'ang* (New Haven, Connecticut: Yale University Press, 1977), p. 242.

16. The "High T'ang" (*sheng T'ang*) period ran roughly from the year of 713, the first year of Emperor Hsüan-tsung's K'ai-yüan reign, to the mid 760's, at the beginning of Emperor Tai-tsung's Ta-li reign. It was a periodization term coined up by literary historians. For a discussion of the term see Stephen Owen's "Introduction" to his *The Great Age of Chinese Poetry: The High T'ang* (New Haven: Yale University Press, 1981), xi-xv.

17. See Hsiao Ti-fei et al. ed. *T'ang-shih chien-shang tz'u-tien* (Shanghai: Tz'u-shu ch'u-pan-she, 1983), pp. 150–51.

18. The story is from the chapter of *T'ang-wen* in the *Liehtzu*. See *Ch'eng-yü tz'u-tien*, p. 254.

19. Wang Wei wrote the biographical stela inscription for Hui-neng (*Neng Ch'an-shih pei*). See *Wang Yu-ch'eng chi chien-chu*, ed. by Chao Tien-ch'eng, (*Ssu-pu pei-yao* ed., 1737, rpt., Shanghai: Chung-hua shu-chü, 4 Vols., undated), *chüan* 25.

20. Cited from Ma Mao-yüan et al. ed., *Ch'u-tz'u chu-shih* (Hsien-ning: Hu-pei jen-min ch'u-pan-she, 1985), p. 477. For David Hawkes's translation see *The Songs of the South*, pp. 206–07. The Blue Waves (*Ts'ang-lang*) is a variant name of the Han river (*Han-shui*) that flows for some 700 miles in central China.

21. The Chinese word for *sorrow* (*ch'ou*), structured as *autumn* (*ch'iu*) over *heart* (*hsin*), has been a favorite pun in Chinese poetic usage. A remarkable example of wordplay on this pun is at the beginning of a lyric song by the Sung *tz'u* master Hsin Ch'i-chi (1140–1207), *To the Tune of Mulberry Picking* (*Ts'ai sang tzu*): "What is sorrow composed of? / Autumn over wayfarer's heart."

5

Scenic Closure in Chinese Literary Criticism

TU FU'S meta-poetic concept of "further space" and "the vast" at the end of a poem, which suggests that a poem's meaning should extend beyond the text's end, had already been recognized for some time as a value in the High T'ang. *Chronicles of T'ang Poetry* (*T'ang-shih chi-shih*), a miscellaneous collection of anecdotes, fragmentary lines, and frequently entire poems of T'ang poets, compiled by Chi Yu-kung of the twelfth century, contains the following record about a poetry contest held in the imperial court in the year 709:

> On the last day of the first month during the reign of [Emperor] Chung-tsung, His Majesty had a gathering for poetic composition at the K'un-ming Pond, and more than one hundred poems were presented by the ministers. In front of the palace hall a decorated tower had been set up for Lady of Bright Countenance, who was commissioned to select one poem to serve as the text for the new imperial song. The ministers waited outside the tower. After a while, slips of paper came flying down, and the ministers picked up their own poems when they found their names on the slips. The only two that had not come down were those by Shen [Ch'üan-ch'i] and Sung [Chih-wen]. After a while, one slip of paper flew down. The ministers raced to snatch it, and found it to be Shen's poem. Later her comments were announced as follows: "The two poems rival each other in craftsmanship. The last lines (*lo chü*) of Shen's poem are: 'This humble courtier, being of withering, rotting stuff / Feels ashamed at sight of the timber of camphor tree.' The poem wears itself out in strength. But Sung's lines are: 'Worry not that the bright moon is gone / As the pearl that shines by night is yet to come.' The poem is still dynamic, as if about to fly up (*chien chü*)." Shen was convinced and argued no more about it.[1]

As the story reveals, the standard of judgment used by the talented imperial concubine, Shang-kuan Wan-erh, in making her final choice between the two best poems in the contest, a criterion that convinced Shen Ch'üan-ch'i, a leading poet of that period, and presumably all those in attendance on that occasion, was focused on poetic closure.

The ending of Shen Ch'üan-ch'i's poem, with its modest reference to himself, falls into the standard closing format of court occasional poems.

This, in Shang-kuan Wan-erh's opinion, "wears itself out in strength." In other words, the meaning of the whole poem has come to an end with the last lines, beyond which nothing is to be further explored semantically. The ending of the poem by Sung Chih-wen, on the other hand, contains two images, a realistic scene (the moonlit night) and a hypothetical scene (the night lit by the legendary pearl). It creates an imaginary world different from that which serves as the background of the poem, and extends the temporal dimension of the poem from the (textual) present into that is yet to come. This was probably what Shang-kuan Wan-erh meant when she noted that the poem was "still dynamic" at its end, "as if about to fly up."

It is irrelevant to our discussion to ascertain the historical truth of the anecdote. The poems of both finalists survive, and it is obvious to any trained reader of Chinese poetry that Sung's poem indeed excels Shen's, precisely in terms of the ending.[2] Shang-kuan Wan-erh, grand-daughter of Shang-kuan Yi, a leading court poet in the seventh century, was not only known as a fine poet herself, but also as a highly respected connoisseur of poetry. Frequently assuming the role of the court arbiter in imperial poetry contest, such as the one described in the above anecdote, she exerted considerable influence on the literary fashion of the period.[3] The record obviously reflects an authoritative critical opinion of early eighth century, a kind of precursor to Tu Fu's meta-poetic comments on poetic closure.

The eighth century in China was an age during which the elaborate civil service examination system reached its maturity. The impact of the incorporation of poetic composition into the system on the development of T'ang poetry has been much discussed, and it is not our concern in this study. However, one text among the numerous "examination poems" (*shih-t'ieh shih*), a poetic sub-genre usually not considered to be of superior literary value in Chinese critical canons, is worth some consideration here, because contemporary discussion of this particular poem reveals much about the appreciation of scenic closure as a poetic device in the High T'ang period.

The text is a famous pentasyllabic poem entitled *The Hsiang Goddesses Playing the Zithers* (*Hsiang-ling ku-she*) by Ch'ien Ch'i, one of the so-called "Ten Prodigies" of the Ta-li period (766–779):

> I often heard that the spirits of the princesses
> Were skillful at playing the zithers from Mount Yün-ho.

P'ing-yi the river god danced to it all by himself,
But the traveler from Ch'u found it no joy to listen.
Rueful melodies flowed mournfully from the instruments,
The clear sound soared high up to distant firmament.
A melancholy longing swept over the plains of Ts'ang-wu,
White angelica stirred, sending out its fragrance.
Flowing waters spread the sound down the river of Hsiao,
Wailing wind sent it on across Lake Tung-t'ing.
When the music ended, no human being was seen,
Along the river loomed a few mountain peaks: so green.[4] (VIII, 2651)

According to another record in the *Chronicles of T'ang Poetry*, this was an examination text submitted by Ch'ien Ch'i, by which he received the advanced degree of the Presented Scholar (*chin-shih*) in the capital in the year of 751. It is a typical examination poem, a pentasyllabic regulated poem in twelve lines, usually with the eight lines in the middle in antithetical couplets, with a limited number of assigned end rhymes, and with its semantic structure developing on the theme of an assigned title.

The poem adheres the general rules of the sub-genre of examination poems in most aspects, including a beginning that immediately refers to the assigned topic, and the use of proper names from or allusions to the precursor *Ch'u-tz'u* text. What made it stand out among the rest of the sub-genre is its closure, which presents an eerie landscape of green mountain peaks looming along the river in the silence. The image seems almost irrelevant to the theme, but it agrees with the folklore around the topic. Since the players of the zithers were supernatural beings, it was only natural that "no human being was seen." The remarkable thing about the closure, though, does not remain with the thematic reference alone. What it has created is a beautiful world in which the sound of the playing of the zithers seems to be lingering over the mountain peaks, long after the music has come to an end. Both the temporal and spatial dimensions of the poem are thus intensified and expanded.

A story about this poem found its way even into the official dynastic history, *The Old History of the T'ang* (*Chiu T'ang shu*):

> [Ch'ien] Ch'i was good at pentasyllabic verse. After he won a nomination from the provincial government [for the imperial examination in the capital], he started leading a traveler's life. Once, on a moonlit night, while putting up at an inn, he was reading poems to himself when he suddenly heard someone chanting in the courtyard: "When the music ended, no human being was seen / Along the river loomed a few mountain peaks: so green." Ch'i was startled;

> he held up his gown and looked outside, but did not see any one there. He thought it must have been from some supernatural being, and he memorized the lines. The year when he took the examination, Li Wei [the Chief Examiner] used *The Hsiang Goddesses Playing the Zithers* as the title for the poetry test, and the word *green* (*ch'ing*) was among the assigned rhyme words. Ch'i thereupon used the lines from the supernatural being to close his poem. Wei liked it very much, and called it supreme. That year Ch'i won the imperial examination.[5]

Although the anecdote might be apocryphal, it probably dated from roughly the same historical period. The fact that such supernatural stories would be invented about the ending of the poem indicates how extraordinary they must have sounded to eighth century readers. In inventing an occasion where such a poetic move could be explained by "what actually happened," this anecdote attempted to give an essentially empirical explanation of a poetic event.

The Chief Examiner Li Wei's criterion in commending this poem was again similar to that of Shang-kuan Wan-erh half a century earlier in terms of its focus on the ending. The reputation of this closure might have played a role in Ch'ien Ch'i's success. Ko Li-fang, a twelfth-century critic, made an interesting observation:

> In the T'ang dynasty many people became famous because of their poetry. Frequently it was only due to one nice poem, or even one polished line, which came to be widely circulated and discussed among celebrities and senior scholars, that the reputation of its author was established. "When the music ended, no human being was seen / Along the river loomed a few mountain peaks: so green." Ch'ien Ch'i became famous because of this.[6]

Indeed Ch'ien Ch'i's fame was to a certain extent established on this poem, which has become one of the most anthologized examination poem, largely because of its suggestive, ethereal closure. That the poem was greatly appreciated and widely considered as a model of its type could also be seen in another related anecdote from the *Chronicles of T'ang Poetry*. More than a century after the composition of Ch'ien Ch'i's poem, one day in the twelfth year (858) of Emperor Hsüan-tsung's reign, while holding the morning court interview, His Majesty raised the issue of the repeated use of the same word in examination texts, and asked his ministers whether it should be considered as a matter of crudity. One of the courtiers, Li Fan, replied that it was an unusual practice, but he nevertheless cited Ch'ien Ch'i's poem, which did use the word *no* (*pu*) twice, as a specimen to argue that the repetition had not prevented the poem from being highly appreciated. The emperor read all the examination poems in Ch'ien Ch'i's year, and afterwards agreed that despite the repetition, Ch'ien Ch'i's poem was indeed the best among them. His Majesty issued an order that the poem be designated as a model text for the candidates in their preparation for the examination.[7]

Some, if not all, of the poems the emperor read in the court that day have survived and been included in *The Complete Poetry of the T'ang* (*chüan* 204). It is interesting to notice that lines that read very much like Ch'ien Ch'i's closing lines are not absent in the texts of the other candidates:

> (Ch'en Chi)
> At one pluck, the new moon becomes white,
> Amid a few strains, the evening mountains turn green. (VI, 2132)
>
> (Wei Ts'ui)
> Through the (zither) pins runs the cold water: blue
> Amid the music, the evening mountains turn green. (VI, 2133)

The similarity between these lines and Ch'ien Ch'i's was of course partially due to the fact that the word *green* (*ch'ing*) was one of the assigned rhyme words in the examination. However, in these two texts, the lines were placed in the fourth couplet, not at the end. Chi Yün, the erudite critic of the Ch'ing dynasty, compared Ch'ien Ch'i's poem with Ch'en Chi's. In his exclusive study of the examination poems, *On the Examination Regulated Poems of T'ang Authors* (*Tang-jen shih-lü shuo*), Chi Yün noted that among all the texts on the topic, Ch'en Chi's was the only one that could be placed next to the great Ch'ien Ch'i poem in its quality. Discussing the similarity between Ch'en Chi's fourth couplet and Ch'ien Ch'i's closure, Chi Yün observed:

> Ch'ien placed the lines at the end of his text, and they thus acquired a spiritual sphere of great distance (*yu yüan shen*). These (Ch'en Chi's lines) were placed in the middle, and they were no more than ordinary good lines.[8]

As Chi Yün further pointed out, what made all the difference was the "arrangement" (*tiao-tu*) at the hand of the poet. The use of image, no matter how refined and vivid, was common practice in Chinese poetry. It was its position, either at the beginning, as in the *Shih-ching* texts, or at the ending in the hand of the T'ang poets, that endowed such images with a force that made them the focus of attention in the poem. Ch'ien Ch'i's closure, different from the closure of the other texts as well as from most of the examination poems of the age, was widely appreciated and even considered the consequence of a supernatural encounter. This seems to further confirm that there was an important change of poetic sensibility in the age, and that Ch'ien Ch'i's lines, generically unusual as they were, were nevertheless embraced by the critical canon of the eighth and ninth centuries.

The focus of attention on poetic closure of that period found another record in the *Secret Book of Literary Mirror*, the handbook of poetic composition compiled by the Kōbō Daishi, *alias* Monk Kūkai, the Japanese Buddhist monk who went to live in China during 802–804. Jumbled as its contents are, the book is nevertheless an invaluable treasure for students of classical Chinese literature, as it has preserved much original material of Early and High T'ang poetics that has disappeared in China. One section of the book, *Seventeen Positions* (*Shih-ch'i shih*), is a discussion of different *shih*, patterns or positions of poetic structure.[9] The tenth position is named the pattern of dropping last lines that contain thought (*han ssu lo chü shih*). It is defined and illustrated as follows:

> The position of dropping last lines that contain (*han*) thought means that the last lines must always be made to hold thought in reserve. One should not let the thought be exhausted when the words come to an end. Sometimes, in the case of a hidden sorrow that can hardly be fully expressed, one should speak of one's mind in the penultimate line, and let the last line describe a sad scene or object which corresponds to the hidden thought. It works well if the thought can emerge and move the reader. [Wang] Ch'ang-ling's *Seeing A Friend Off* says: "Drunk, I cannot utter a single word / Over the fields and hills, a rain mists." Another example of last lines: "I look for miraculous herbs, from morning till dark / The empty mountains are fragrant, with pines and cassias." And yet another: "The villages yonder are the Huai county / Beneath a long smoke, beside brooks and trees." One more example from Li Chan's poem: "How is this mind ever going to settle down? / Beneath the new moon lies the river, clear and long."[10]

An important concept about poetic closure in this passage revolves around the term *han* in the text, the meaning of which approximates the English word *contain*: to hold within or to enclose; there is also a hint of withholding or reserving something in the Chinese term. What is suggested here is the dichotomy of an exterior or surface (*wai*) and an interior or depth (*nei*), which had already emerged in Chinese literary and critical consciousness for some time by the High T'ang period. Since the ending is supposed to *contain* thought, then, obviously, it is not supposed to be an explicit, open statement of thought. Instead the thought is to be hidden within. If so, what is to be displayed on the surface? This passage suggests that the way is to use a scene or an object (*ching wu*) which somehow relates to the inner thought. One remarkable point about the examples cited in this passage is that they all include a penultimate line that either refers to or directly declares the mind or thought (although in the first example what the line discusses is actually silence, not speaking), whereas the subsequent last line always presents a scene or an image. In other words, the closure consists of a factual statement followed by a descriptive non-statement.

In another section of the *Literary Mirror*, it is once again suggested that the last lines should make one feel that the thought has not yet been fully expressed at the poem's end. The example cited is the closure of a poem by Ch'en Tzu-ang: "The road leads henceforth into the threshold of Shu / Clouds and mountains spread wide and far." It is argued in this passage, just as in the previous one, that the closure should leave further room for thought, and that the use of a scene at a poem's ending is exemplary. If we compare these examples with those T'ang poems with scenic closure as discussed in previous chapters, the similarity is obvious. From these passages, as well as from Tu Fu's meta-poetic lines and the anecdote about Shang-kuan Wan-erh's arbitration, a distant horizon of literary expectations and values emerges.

The argument in the *Secret Book of Literary Mirror*, that the best way to extend the thought of a poem at its end is to use an object or scene, involves the relation between the *ch'ing* (emotion) and the *ching* (scene), or *wu* (external object) in earlier usage, which has been an essential part of traditional Chinese poetics.

In contrast to Western poetics that started with an emphasis on *mimesis*, i.e., an imitation or representation of the external world, early Chinese literary criticism focused on the internal human mind that conceives and seeks expression of itself. "Poetry (*shih*) tells what is in one's mind (*chih*)," says a line from *The Book of Documents* (*Shang-shu*), one of the oldest classics in Chinese history.[11] The *Great Preface* to *Mao's Scholia* of the *Shih-ching* also contains the following often cited statement:

> Poetry comes from what's in one's mind (*chih*). When it is in one's mind it is called the *chih*; when it is expressed in words it becomes poetry (*shih*). Emotions (*ch'ing*) stir inside, and take shape in words.[12]

Although both the *chih* and *ch'ing* were mentioned in this passage, throughout the Han dynasty the former term acquired a heavy ethical and political meaning, and was often used in the sense of *aspiration* or *will*. It was also favored over the latter in critical and literary usages. By the third century, probably as a deviation from the orthodox Confucian ideology officially promoted since the second century B.C., and based on the flourish of lyrical poetry in the form of the pentasyllabic verse, Lu Chi suggested that "poetry comes from emotions," thus reaffirming the importance of expressing basic human emotions in poetry, as had been demonstrated in Chinese literature since the *Shih-ching*.[13]

Aspiration or emotion, the expression of mind alone does not constitute poetic creativity. In Chinese culture human being has always been considered an integral part of the larger world. *Notes on Music* (*Yüeh-chi*), a work that was probably produced in the Warring States period, made an early dialectic observation of the relation between human mind (*hsin*) and external things or objects (*wu*):

> Music comes from human mind. It is the external things that set human mind in motion. Touched by external things, human mind stirs and forms into sounds...When emotions are stirred up inside, they take shape in sounds; when the sounds form into a pattern, they become music.[14]

Like music, all arts come from the interaction of human mind and things in the world. In the ultimate sense, without the myriad things in the world, human mind can hardly hope to be activated and consequently to find its expression in any art form. Poetry does tell what is in one's mind, but just as demonstrated by examples from earliest Chinese poetry, particularly poems from the *Shih-ching*, poetry is not simply the statement of what is in one's mind. Consider the following lines from the famous song, No. 167 (*Ts'ai wei*), in the *Hsiao-ya* section from the *Shih-ching*:

> Erstwhile, when I left,
> The willows were soft and tender.
> Now, when I come back,
> It abounds with snow and rain.

The late Ch'ing critic Liu Hsi-tsai used this stanza as an illustration of his observation on the importance of the scene (*ching*) in poetry. He remarked:

> A poet's strong appeal lies precisely in his revealing the emotions through the scene. Here, if the scenes were excluded, then what it says would be simply: "I left in spring, and return in winter." Would it then have any savor at all?[15]

Obviously, to reduce those lines to "I left in spring and return in winter" would be excluding what is essentially beautiful in poetry. In Liu Hsi-tsai's argument, then, poetry comes from the interrelation and interaction, or rather the fusion (*chiao-jung*), of two essential elements: human mind and external things. The anonymous singers of the *Shih-ching* poems, even though they were unlikely to be aware of the concept in a critical sense, embodied it in their own composition.

As demonstrated in the citations above, as early as in the pre-Ch'in and Han periods the relation between *mind* and *world* already caught some critical attention, vague and fragmentary as it was. By the fourth and fifth centuries, with the increasing influence of literature as a self-conscious creative activity, the relation was further explored by Chinese literati. Lu Chi, in his *Wen-fu*, has touched upon the topic while discussing the difficulties of creative writing: "I always worry that the idea (*yi*) may not agree with the object (*wu*), and that the writing (*wen*) may fail to express the idea."[16] As the contemporary Chinese scholar Ch'ien Chung-shu has observed, this statement implies a dichotomy between an external surface in the term *object*, and an inner depth in the term *idea*. The writing, the literary text, is regarded as something that comes from that inner depth, but manifests itself on the external surface: it is considered a convergence of both. These three (idea, object, and text), according to the description in the *Wen-fu*, form a kind of trirelative or a tripod in relation.[17] Lu Chi further described the creative process:

> Going through the four seasons, he sighs at the fleeting time;
> Looking at the myriad things, he is filled with thoughts.
> He grieves over falling leaves in grim autumn;
> He delights in the tender shoots of sweet spring.

Here Lu Chi seems to have placed his emphasis on the influence of natural phenomena or things in nature on human emotions. Liu Hsieh's

Wen-hsin tiao-lung also concentrated on the relation between emotion and nature in literature. In the chapter entitled "The Aspects of Things" (*Wu se*), he elaborated on Lu Chi's idea: "Spring and autumn come in alternation. The *yin* and the *yang* make us miserable and cheerful by turns. The changes in the aspects of things set our mind in motion."[18] As the Japanese scholar Kōzen Hiroshi has observed, in Liu Hsieh's usage as well as in the usage of his time, the term *wu se* referred in particular to things in nature or natural phenomena.[19] However, on other occasions in the book the term *wu* may include all kinds of things in the world outside the human mind, as in the chapter of "Explaining Poetry" (*Ming shih*): "Man is endowed with the seven emotions; in response to the external things they are set in motion. Being stirred up by things, man sings about what is in his mind; this is only natural." (VI, 48) Even though Liu Hsieh's work was for a long time ignored by the literati, and hence did not have much influence on the T'ang poets, it is nevertheless notable that the significance of leaving something beyond the text was not unrecognized in his age, some two centuries before the High T'ang era. Liu Hsieh argued that in describing nature or landscape, it would be most desirable to have the emotions still lingering after the description has come to an end (XLVI, 494). In explaining his term *yin* (the latent) as "the layered meaning that lies beyond the text" (*wen-wai chih ch'ung-chih*) (XL, 431), Liu Hsieh showed himself to be a forerunner of the numerous later Chinese critics who discussed the concept of "reserve / accumulation within" (*han-hsü*), i.e., withholding and storing something within the text.[20] On another occasion Liu Hsieh observed: "As for the subtle messages beyond one's thinking, and the complex idea outside the text, they are what language cannot overtake and what the writing brush knows well when to give up." (XXVI, 296) This observation seems to indicate that Liu Hsieh was concerned with the issue of how best and when to put an end to a literary text. Liu Hsieh also made an even more specific remark on the closure of a literary text:

> As for putting down one's writing brush and closing the text, it can be compared to raising one's oars while riding in a boat; and as for making the words unify in the right order, it is like drawing in the reins and brandishing the horsewhip. To achieve completion at the end, one should make it profound and write down something as if seeing someone off.[21] (XLIII, 463)

Fragmentary and sometimes dubious in meaning as these comments were, it is not difficult to perceive in them a similar concern with closure that they shared with the T'ang poets from Shang-kuan Wan-erh to Tu Fu. Chung Hung, a contemporary of Liu Hsieh's, whose *Categories of Poets* (*Shih-p'in*) reached a larger audience than the *Wen-hsin tiao-lung* in the next few centuries, also realized the important relation of mind and world: "The vital force (*ch'i*) activates things (*wu*). Things move people. Thus when emotions and feelings are stirred, they find their expression in dancing and singing."[22] Unlike Lu Chi and Liu Hsieh who concentrated on nature, Chung Hung included both natural and social phenomena in his concept of objects or things (*wu*) as the motivating force of human emotions.

Although little from the critical writings of T'ang writers survives today, it is clear that the attention to the relation of these two elements was still a part of the critical sensibility of the time. This is confirmed by the passages on two of the *Seventeen Positions* from the *Secret Book of Literary Mirror*:

> The position of reasoning incorporated into scene (*li ju ching*): Poetry should not be entirely reasoning. Instead it should be incorporated into a scene; only then will the lines be savory.
>
> The position of scene incorporated into reasoning (*ching ju li*): Poetry, if it talks only about ideas (*yi*), is turbid [in style] and tasteless. If it talks only about scene, it is also tasteless. It would be a nice event (*shih*) to include both scene and ideas. When words of scene are incorporated into words of reasoning, they must agree with each other. The ideas should be held tight rather than directly expressed.[23]

The writers of the Sung dynasty further clarified the relation in their critical consciousness on the basis of previous observations on the relation between the object and the mind, and most likely, also from their admiration for the brilliant practice of T'ang poets, which found such rich and various ways of artistic expression for an "incorporation" of one into the other. In a dialogue with Ou-yang Hsiu, the poet Mei Yao-ch'en remarked:

> One must be able to depict scenes which are difficult to describe, and make them look as if they were right in front of one's eyes; one must be able to contain unending meanings, and have them emerge somewhere beyond words. Only then will perfection be achieved.

When Ou-yang Hsiu demanded some illustrations of the idea, Mei

Yao-ch'en said it was hard to define in words, as it was something that the author and the reader perceived respectively in each of their mind. Nevertheless he did cite a few couplets from T'ang poets as examples:

> In the pond beneath willows, spring waters overflow;
> At the flowery cove, the evening sun comes late.
>
> The cocks crowed: the moon was over the thatched inn;
> Footprints were left on the frosted wooden bridge.
>
> Strange birds were screaming in the wilderness;
> The setting sun was frightening to the wayfarers.

All these lines, as Mei Yao-ch'en explained, are descriptions of scenes which hold some deep emotions and ideas in reserve within the poem, either the leisurely enchantment in fine springtime as revealed in the first couplet, or the distress and hardship of the people wandering away from home.[24]

In discussing Tu Fu's poetry, Fan Hsi-wen, a thirteenth century Sung critic, identified different examples of "emotion within scene," "scene within emotion," and "the indistinguishable convergence of emotion and scene." He therefore came to this conclusion: "Scene, without emotion, will not arise; and emotion, without scene, will not surface."[25]

The concept was occasionally discussed in the Sung dynasty, but it became a perennially favorite topic through the Ming and Ch'ing eras, most notably in the works of Hsieh Chen and Wang Fu-chih. Emotion and scene were not only clearly defined as the two essentials of poetry, but also as a pair of *binary oppositions*, the two sides of one unity; and poetry was considered the expression of such a unity. As Wang Fu-chih has argued, although emotion is related with the *self* (*wo*), and scene is related with the *world* (*wu*), and they are called by two different names, they are actually inseparable. To cite the nice metaphor from Wang: emotion and scene "lie hidden in each other's lodging" (*hu ts'ang ch'i chai*).[26]

Such "fusion of emotion and scene" (*ch'ing ching chiao-jung*) is precisely what lies in the art of the T'ang poets in their use of scenic closure. Such closure consists of not mere images, but rather images endowed with emotions and ideas which, though not made explicit in the text, nevertheless stay in reserve within. These images are used, and often work well, at other positions in the structure of a text, but somehow they work most admirably as endings, according to classical Chinese poetics since the High T'ang. This is probably because at that position, images as such may extend the dimensions of the poem by leaving behind them a space laden with meanings, and thus enable the poem to "join the vast" as Tu Fu suggested, at its very end.

Views on poetic closure close to Tu Fu's meta-poetic commentary may be found in the few late Tang works of poetics that exist today. The Buddhist monk Ch'i Chi, a fine poet himself, included among his "Six Types of Closure" (*liu tuan*) one of "unending idea" (*pu chin yi*), which he illustrated by the lines: "I'll speak my mind out only when we meet / I often climb the tower to look at distant mountains."[27] In this example, we are again reading a penultimate line that makes a statement, paradoxical as it is (what it is saying is in fact "I will not speak out my mind now"), to be succeeded by the last line which seems to be flying off at a tangent, i.e., talking about something else that apparently has little connection with the previous line. Like Wang Ch'ang-ling's lines quoted as the first example of the tenth position in the *Seventeen Positions*, as above cited, the penultimate line discusses silence, not sound or speech. Likewise, the last line also makes a spatial extension, as scenic closure frequently does. Hsü Yin, a writer who won the *chin-shih* degree in the last decade of the ninth century, also remarked that "the ending must have some unending idea, to be accumulated behind it, some idea that stays lingering there."[28]

Such concept about poetic closure was continued through the Sung dynasty. Wen Yü, a Buddhist monk of the tenth century, insisted that poetic closure, or in his words "poetic tail" (*shih wei*) or the "amputating line" (*tuan chü*) must "hold in reserve" (*han-hsü*) a certain "gusto" (*chih ch'ü*).[29] Throughout the Sung there was a strong critical interest in poetic closure. This probably explained why Tu Fu's *Song of Fowls-Trussing* became one of the most widely discussed poems in the period.[30]

Some sophisticated remarks related to poetic closure in the late Sung period were from Chiang K'uei, the great lyric-song (*tz'u*) poet as well as a *shih* poet. His *White Stone Taoist's Remarks on Poetry* (*Pai-shih Tao-jen shih-shuo*) is a brief and fragmentary collection of frequently insightful comments. The following are some of Chiang K'uei's observations on poetic closure: "If the text's ending (*p'ien chung*) can take people by surprise, or reverse the meaning of the whole text, it is wonderful." He also stressed the importance of *han-hsü*: "Writing should aim at holding something in reserve." He cited the words of the Northern Sung poet Su Shih to make his point: "Those in which the words have an end but the meanings are endless are the best writings in the world." He favored extended dimensions in a literary text: "Sentences that have a lingering flavor, texts that have lingering meanings, these are the best of all." Like Fan Hsi-wen, Chiang K'uei regarded emotion and scene as a complementary pair: "Scene is to be contained in idea; idea is to be contained in scene." In particular he underscored the importance of poetic ending: "A [poetic] text relies completely on its last line."[31]

Chiang K'uei's idea found a parallel in that of Shen Yi-fu, an important *tz'u* theoretician from the same period, who said in his work on various issues of the composition of the lyric-song (despite its title), *Guidebook for Music Bureau Poetry* (*Yüeh-fu chih-mi*): "The closing line must let loose (*fang k'ai*), holding some unending idea in reserve. The best way is to close in emotions with a scene (*yi ching chieh ch'ing*)."[32] Scenic closure was now clearly defined as a poetic device, "the best way," to achieve the art of *han hsü* or "holding thoughts in reserve." Incidentally, the observations on poetic closure of Chiang K'uei and Shen Yi-fu were made largely on the basis of the practice of the lyric-song poets, wherein the scenic closure was widely used. Sometimes a lyric-song poet become widely known because of a famous line or closure, or even won an appellation derived from that line or closure, as in the case of Ho Chu, a major lyric-song writer of the Northern Sung period (960-1126). He was known as "Ho the Plum (*Prunus mume*) Fruit" because of the closing lines of his song "To the Tune of *Path to the Horizontal Pond*" (*Heng-t'ang lu*):

May I ask: how deep is your sorrow in idleness?
    A plain far and wide, covered in misty grass;
    All over the city, willow catkins fly in the wind;
    The rain that drizzles when plum fruits turn yellow.

Following the rhetorical question which is not superseded with a direct reply, the closure presents a whole set of scenes integrated with emotions. It was widely admired by Ho Chu's contemporaries.[33] It should also be noted here that the stanzaic structure, which had faded out since the *Shih-ching*, made its comeback with the rise of the lyric-song, though a remarkable difference between the new song forms and the ancient texts was the shifting dominant position of the affective image (*hsing*). In the ancient anthology, it was generally used at the beginning of a stanza; with the new forms, it was widely used at the end.[34]

There have been various terms for poetic closure in Chinese literary criticism. The most popular term through the T'ang seemed to be *tuan chü*, literally "the line that breaks off or amputates."[35] Others used were the body term of *wei chü* ("tail line") or the *lo chü* ("dropping line"), both of which carried some sense of closure. Shen Yi-fu was among a few to use the term *chieh chü* ("ending line"). Different as the names are, great scenic closure, that of the great T'ang poets and the Sung lyric-song poets, should not considered *closure* in the Western sense of the word. It does not *close*, but rather *opens* to more space. It does not conclude, but leave questions unanswered. It does not complete the poems, but enhance the significance of the poems by staying incomplete. A characteristic of Chinese poetry lies precisely in its incompleteness, often as a result of the use of scenic closure.

The perennial debate on the closure of *The Old Fisherman* (*Yü-weng*), a short heptasyllabic poem by Liu Tsung-yüan, can serve as an illustration of the critical attention on this issue. The poem runs as follows:

> The old fisherman slept by night beneath the western cliff,
> At dawn drew water from the clear Hsiang and made fire with the bamboo of
> Ch'u.
> Mist vanished, the sun came out; no one was seen around.
> Amid sound of the swinging scull, mountains and waters were so green.
> Look back at the skyline: it was going down the midstream;
> Over the cliff, mindless, the clouds were in pursuit. (XI, 3957)

On the surface this is a simple descriptive poem. The first line tells us about a human figure (*the old fisherman*), the time (*by night*), and the spatial location (*beneath the western cliff*) of the scene. What is left unsaid but somewhat hinted (from the fact that the character is a fisherman) is that the location must be at or close to the riverside.

In the second line this is clarified: it is the river Hsiang, which flows through the southwestern provinces of Kwangsi (where Liu was sent on exile at the time) and Hunan. In Liu Tsung-yüan's lifetime such proper names like the Hsiang and Ch'u (as used in the second line) would immediately give the reader of the central part of China with a sense of the exotic, with all the associations of such exiled poets like Ch'ü Yüan and Chia Yi and their poems. Unlike Wang Wei's poem, *In Reply to District Defender Chang*, which also includes a fisherman in its description, Liu's poem seems to have no apparent political message in its use of the fisherman, at least not at the beginning. Besides the geographical allusion, the second line also presents a close shot of the fisherman's activities. The ordinary act of cooking (drawing water and lighting up a fire) is somewhat defamiliarized through the combined use of exotic geographic names. Time has also changed from that in the beginning: the night is over, and it is now daybreak.

Time continues moving on: in the third line the sunshine dispels the morning mist, the reader can expect to extend his vision, not such a close view as presented in the second line, but where is the fisherman now? An answer is hinted at in the next line, which presents an auditory image as well as a visual one, indicating that the fisherman is already out somewhere down the river (from the sound of the scull). Although the word *green* does not appear until now, the color has been an underlying suggestion since the beginning, in the references to the cliff, the river, the bamboo. In this line, just as in Ch'ien Ch'i's closure that we have discussed earlier, there is a seemingly irrelevant combination of sound and vision.

Up till now the text has been apparently noncommittal description. With the next two lines, the poem becomes somewhat confusing. The confusion lies partially in the Chinese syntax which does not necessarily require a subject for the predicate in a sentence. (In my translation above I have tried deliberately to retain the ambiguity in the original.) While the fourth line does not specify where the fisherman exactly is, except hinting by the sound of the scull that he is probably rowing his little boat somewhere, the fifth line gives some further suggestion: he is already in the far distance, probably in the boat "going down the midstream." The term *mindless* (*wu hsin*) reminds one of the symbolic lines from T'ao Ch'ien's famous rhyme-prose composition, *Homeward Bound* (*Kuei-ch'ü-lai tz'u*): "The clouds have no mind to come out of the valley; / The birds, tired with flying, know well when to return." But somehow the allusion does not work well here, because there is nothing in the previous lines that agrees with or complements it. Questions arise: Who is "looking back" at the distant horizon? Who is looking upwards at the clouds over the cliff? Who makes the assumption that the clouds are *mindless*? Is it the old fisherman, as generally understood? Is it the author himself? Or is it some bystander? With the last two lines, noncommittal objectivity abruptly yields to subjectivity.

Su Shih, the leading poet and central literary figure of the Northern Sung, was the first to suggest that the poem would be a better one without the last two lines. There were a few dissenting voices, such as those of Liu Ch'en-weng, a Southern Sung poet, and the poets Li Tung-yang and Wang Shih-chen of the Ming dynasty. But most later poets and critics sided with Su Shih. Yen Yü, for example, asserted that even if Liu Tsung-yüan came back to life again he would heartily approve of Su Shih's suggestion. The early Ch'ing poet Wang Shih-chen simply called the last two lines of the poem the result of "drawing a snake and adding feet to it," an unnecessary addition, and accused those defending the two lines as "blind."[36]

The lasting debate about the poem seems to have focused on the issue of completeness and incompleteness, revealing basic difference in aesthetic taste and evaluation. The last two lines appear to have completed the poem by providing further explanation to questions raised in the third line: "Why was there no one to be seen around? Where was the fisherman?" The answers to these questions cannot be found in the fourth line. Now they are addressed in the fifth line: the fisherman is "going down the midstream." The last line, besides providing insinuation of a possible political message with the T'ao Ch'ien's term of *mindless*, makes a cyclical movement towards the beginning and rounds the poem up by referring back to the *cliff* mentioned in the first line.

It is precisely the last two lines, it seems to this reader, that weakens the lyrical effects of the poem, making it a mid-T'ang rather than a High T'ang text. As Stephen Owen has so convincingly observed through his close reading of a number of texts from both periods: "the High T'ang poet gives the impression of having said less than he might, while the mid-T'ang poet often gives the impression of having said more than he ought."[37]

Had the poem ended at the fourth line as Su Shih suggested, the text would have created a self-contained poetic world. With the fourth line as its closure, with its combination of auditory and visual images, the poem would have looked incomplete, but it would enable the text to "join the vast," to leave much room for the reader to meditate on. The poem would have enjoyed an intensified compactness by leaving its semantic content incomplete. As it is, the fifth and sixth lines of the poem dramatize the scene with the intrusion of a subjective mind. It is as if someone had abruptly imposed himself between the scene and the spectator, trying in an uncouth manner to give his most unwelcome and misleading interpretation. What emerges as a result of such enactment is a sense of disharmony and bathos. That the majority of Chinese literati, poets and critics alike, would stand by Su Shih, is not surprising. This reveals that the appreciation of scenic closure as a poetic device to achieve a certain incompleteness, or rather to withhold an "unended idea" (to use Ch'i Chi's term), is very much a part of mainstream Chinese poetics. The gesture of allegiance, such as that given by later poets and critics in support of Su Shih's opinion, was actually the victory of the High T'ang poetry as an unchanging model and repository of value.

Yu-kung Kao and Tsu-lin Mei, in an illuminating short essay on the early Ch'ing poet Wang Shih-chen that quite unusually focuses on his poetic closure, have discussed Wang's closing devices of what they call "image in suspension" and the "solution unresolved," which "create a sense of complexity and uncertainty.[38] They have perceptively attributed the use of such devices to Wang Shih-chen's commitment to the tradition of the past, especially that of the T'ang period, and his search for the "secret methods of poetry composition" of what constituted excellence in regulated verse. Their discovery provides another evidence of how the scenic closure, firmly established at the hands of the High T'ang poets, has become an integral part of classical Chinese poetry and poetics.

Why should a line of image be considered artistically superior to a line of thought? Why should a non-statement regarded as being capable of speaking more than a statement? At the back of the aesthetics of scenic closure lies the suspicion of language in Chinese philosophical tradition.

The story about the Wheelwright Pien in the *Book of Chuangtzu* is a fine example of that suspicion:

> Huan-kung (Duke of Ch'i) was reading in the hall. Wheelwright Pien, who was cutting a wheel outside the hall, put aside his hammer and chisel, came up into the hall, and asked Huan-kung, "May I take the liberty to ask what kind of words you are reading here?" The duke said, "These are the words of the sages." The wheelwright said, "Are these sages still alive?" The duke said, "They are dead." The Wheelwright said, "Then what you are reading are only the dregs of the ancients." Huan-kung said, "While I, your lord, am reading, how dare a wheel-maker make any comments? If you have a reason it is all right; if you cannot give a reason, then you'll die!" Wheelwright Pien said, "I, your humble servant, tend to look at things in terms of my own job. When one

cuts a wheel, if one goes too slowly, it slides and does not stick fast; if one cuts too quickly, it resists and does not go in. The way to do it is neither too slowly nor too quickly. One learns it in one's mind, and one's hands respond to that. Although it cannot be put in words, there is some underlying principle. I cannot make it known to my son, nor can my son inherit it from me. I am about to be seventy years old, and I'll grow old in cutting wheels. The ancients have died, and that cannot be transmitted have died with them. Therefore I say that what you are reading are the dregs of the ancients!"[39]

Although the fable was originally used to illustrate the argument that the great *Heavenly Way* (*T'ien tao*) was something beyond human language (which at its most could hope to convey only traces of "shape, color, name, and sound"), there developed from it the idea that the complexity of life and world is something that can never be fully expressed in words.

Another ancient story, included in *Lü's Spring and Autumn Annals* (*Lü-shih ch'un-ch'iu*), demonstrates a similar doubt of language as the vehicle for communication. One day Yi Yin, the Shang minister who was also known as an excellent chef, entertained Ch'eng-t'ang, the king, with a dinner. When the king praised the food, Yi Yin observed that the Way (*tao*) was like the extreme deliciousness of the food in the pot, something not to be expressed in words nor conveyed through mind.[40]

Throughout later centuries these stories have exerted their influence on Chinese literary criticism. The influence may be traced in works from Lu Chi's *Wen-fu* and Liu Hsieh's *Wen-hsin tiao-lung* all the way to the early Ch'ing poet Wang Shih-chen's theory of "spirit and tone" (*shen yün*) and Wang Kuo-wei's concept of the "artistic world" (*ching-chieh*).

The late T'ang poet Ssu-k'ung T'u used concrete images to stand for a number of abstract, subtle stylistic modes in his *Twenty-four Categories of Poetry* (*Erh-shih-ssu shih-p'in*). Yen Yü, the Sung critic, carried on the torch of this somewhat mystic school of literary criticism, maintaining that the ultimate achievement of poetry was in "entering the realm of spirit" (*ju shen*):

Poetry involves a particular material that has nothing to do with books. Poetry involves a particular interest that has nothing to do with reason ... What makes the very best involves the saying: "Neither set one's foot upon the path of reason, nor fall into the trap of words." ... The High T'ang poets relied entirely on their inspiring savor (*hsing ch'ü*), like an antelope that hangs [on the branches of trees] by its horns, leaving no trace to be pursued. The marvel of their poetry is in its transparency and delicacy, that refuse to be assembled, like sound in the air, color in a face, moonlight in water, or reflection in a mirror.

> The words may be exhausted, but the meaning is boundless.[41]

The rise of the Ch'an Buddhism, which stressed the impossibility of communication through language, also further exerted an influence on such suspicion of language came from. The Ch'an riddle (*gatha*), which rose to fashion in the T'ang and reached its peak in the Sung, often used images for complex ideas, aiming at grasping the truth of things intuitively rather than conceptually. While its impact could already be perceived in the poetry of a High T'ang poet like Wang Wei, it became most obvious in the works of such Sung poets as Su Shih and Huang T'ing-chien, the latter being widely considered during the Sung as a master of using scenic closure in the tradition of Tu Fu.[42]

All such exploration for truth or reality beyond words accounts for the appreciation of scenic closure as a way to express some otherwise inexpressible ideas. Scenic closure, as mentioned above, does not consist of an image alone. To repeat Wang Fu-chih's metaphor, it is emotions lying hidden in the lodging of scene. It is an image that is impregnated with emotions not made explicit at the ending. Nor is it a *closing* of conclusion, as it aims at *opening* to a world beyond words.

The paradox of such suspicion of language is that, after all, the suspicion itself still has to be defined in language. The paradox of the scenic closure lies in that in the final sense, it does not have an autonomous life of its own. In the light of Wang Shih-chen's theory of the "spirit and tone," the scenic closure can well be understood as that part of the poem which creates and enhances all that *spirit* and *tone*. But, just as Ch'ien Chung-shu has noticed in his discussion of Wang Shih-chen's theory:

> Since it is the spirit, it is different from body; and since it is tone it is different from sound. Yet the spirit can only be felt when it is within a body, and the tone can only be discerned in its accompaniment to the sound.[43]

In other words, the scenic closure is not complete in itself. It is only a part of the fabric of the poetic text, not the entirety of its intricate texture. All those image endings that have been discussed above, wonderful as they are, would be insignificant outside their respective contexts. It is the very position where they are placed that provides them with all their artistic charm and strength.

Notes

1. See Wang Chung-yung ed., *T'ang-shih chi-shih chiao-chien* (Ch'engtu: Pa-Shu shu-she, 2 Vols., 1989), I, *chüan* 3, p. 50. The same story is also found in *Ch'üan T'ang shih-hua*, attributed to the Southern Sung poet Yu Mao (1127–94). See Ho Wen-huan ed., *Li-tai shih-hua* (Peking: Chung-hua shu-chü, 2 Vols., 1981), I, p. 62. In the *Ssu-k'u ch'üan-shu tsung-mu t'i-yao* the latter *shih-hua* was attributed to Liao Ying-chung, a retainer under Chia Shih-tao (1213–75), the thirteenth century Sung Prime Minister; it is considered of less value because much of it directly borrowed from Chi Yu-kung's work. The former is now generally regarded as a book of great documentary value in its preservation of a great amount of original T'ang material. See the *Introduction* to *Li-tai shih-hua*, I, p. 1. See also Kuo Shao-yü, *Sung shih-hua k'ao* (Peking: Chung-hua shu-chü, 1979), pp. 73–75, 121–25. Emperor Chung-tsung was enthroned in 683, but ruled only for one year before he was deposed by Wu Tse-t'ien (624–705), who later made herself Empress (ruled 690–705). Chung-tsung was restored in 705, and ruled until he was poisoned to death in 710. Lady of Bright Countenance (*Chao-jung*) was the official title for one of the Nine Imperial Concubines; in this case it was Shang-kuan Wan-erh (664–710), well known for her poetic talent. K'un-ming Pond, a man-made lake in the suburbs of Ch'ang-an, was constructed by order of the Martial Emperor of Han in the year of 120 B.C, to use for naval exercises and to provide a water source for the capital. When it was first built, it was said to be more than five thousand acres in area and have a circumference of about 120 miles. It had gradually dried out since early fifth century, was dredged and rebuilt in 797, but dried up again during early ninth century.

2. Both texts are in *Ch'üan T'ang shih* (Shanghai: Chung-hua shu-chü, 25 Vols., 1985). Sung Chih-wen's poem is in II, p. 647; Shen Ch'üan-ch'i's is in IV, p. 1045. All further citations of T'ang poems, with the volume number and pagination noted parenthetically within the text, are from this edition.

3. Chi Yu-kung, *T'ang-shih chi-shih* (Shanghai: Chung-hua shu-chü, 2 Vols., 1965), I, *chüan* 3, pp. 25–29.

4. The title of this poem had its origin in the *Far-off Journey* (*Yüan-yu*), a long poem about an imaginary journey in *The Songs of the South* (*Ch'u-tz'u*). Two lines from the poem runs thus: "I made the Hsiang Goddesses pluck their zithers / And I bade Hai-jo (sea god) dance with P'ing-yi." For a complete translation of the poem see David Hawkes, *The Songs of the South*, pp. 191–203. According to one source in the ancient book of folklore, *Book of Mountains and Seas* (*Shan-hai-ching*), the legendary sage-king Yao married his two daughters to his successor Shun. After Shun's death the two wives lived in the Chiu-yi mountains, and later became the goddesses of the Hsiang, hence the reference in the poem to "spirits of the princesses." Ts'ang-wu was a place in Southern China where Shun was said to have been buried. The "traveler from Ch'u" is a reference to the attributed author of the text in *The Songs of the South*.

5. See *Chiu T'ang shu*, *chüan* 168 (Shanghai: Chung-hua shu-chü, 16 Vols., 1975), XIII, pp. 4382–83. For a similar record with some slight variation see *T'ang-shih chi-shih chiao-chien*, I, *chüan* 30, p. 832.

6. Ko Li-fang, *Yün-yü yang-ch'iu*, *chüan* 4. See *Li-tai shih-hua*, II, pp. 516–17.

7. Chi, *Tang-shih chi-shih*, I, *chüan* 2, pp. 20–21.

8. Chi Yün, *T'ang-jen shih-lü shuo* (1759, revised 1760), from *Kuo-ch'ao ming-jen chu-shu ts'ung-shu* (Shanghai: Sung-yin ko, 10 Vols., 1879), IX, pp. 16b–17b.

9. For an explanation of the Chinese critical term *shih* see Owen, *Readings*, pp. 590–91.

10. Wang Li-ch'i ed., *Wen-ching mi-fu-lun chiao-chu* (Peking: Chung-kuo she-hui k'o-hsüeh ch'u-pan-she, 1983), pp. 128–29. The section of *Seventeen Positions*, like a few other sections, was attributed to the famous poet Wang Ch'ang-ling (698–757) in several early manuscripts of the book. Kūkai wrote elsewhere that he obtained, from some poet during his stay in China, a copy of Wang Ch'ang-ling's *Poetic Structure* (*Shih-ko*) in one *chüan*. He also mentioned that, although there were several works bearing the same title, "the talents of the age were in great favor of this one in particular." The contents of these sections, however, are markedly different from the now existent *Poetic Structure* attributed to Wang Ch'ang-ling, but very close to *The Secret Purports in Poetry* (*Shih-chung mi-chih*), a work generally attributed to the mid-T'ang poet Chia Tao (779–843), but according to another argument attributed to Wang Ch'ang-ling, as included in the *Yin-ch'uang tsa-lu*. From these texts, Wang Li-ch'i argued that the existent *Poetic Structure* must be a later forgery, and that the citations of Wang Ch'ang-ling in the *Literary Mirror*, including this section, constitute the original *Poetic Structure* obtained by Kūkai. However, Kūkai was in China almost half a century after the death of Wang Ch'ang-ling; hence even the *Poetic Structure* that Kūkai personally obtained could still be a forged work attributed to the poet, who enjoyed an extremely high fame even in his own lifetime. However, there is no doubt it was from an authentic work of High T'ang poetics. The next citation from the book is on p. 307, also attributed to Wang Ch'ang-ling in some manuscripts of the book.

11. This is a citation from the section of *Yao-tien* in the *Shang-shu*. See Kuo and Wang, I, p. 1. Chu Tzu-ch'ing (1898–1948) has observed in his *Shih-yen-chih pien* that this line from the *Shang-shu* is the "ground-breaking" principle of all Chinese literary criticism. See *Chu Tzu-ch'ing ku-tien wen-hsüeh lun-wen-chi* (Shanghai: Ku-chi ch'u-pan-she, 2 Vols., 1981), Vol. I, p. 190. As mentioned in Kuo and Wang, I, p. 1, Note 9, when quoted by Ssu-ma Ch'ien in the *Shih-chi* (in the *Wu-ti pen-chi*), the term *chih* is replaced by the word *yi* (*idea*). Chu Tzu-ch'ing has observed that in Han terminology the two were almost identical. See p. 194.

12. Kuo and Wang, I, p. 63.

13. See Chang Shao-k'ang, *Wen-fu chi-shih* (Shanghai: Ku-chi ch'u-pan-she, 1984), p. 71. Read also Note 8 on pp. 77–80. This work represents the best recent scholarship on Lu Chi's *Wen-fu* from the Chinese mainland. Chang Shao-k'ang has convincingly argued that the term *ch'ing* in the context is used in its general sense referring to the "seven emotions," i.e., joy, anger, sorrow, fear, love, hate, and desire. However, as Chu Tzu-ch'ing has remarked, the *Shang-shu* principle and Lu Chi's concept were sometimes considered to be conflicting ideas throughout Chinese literary criticism since the Six Dynasties: the former representing an ethical, ideological approach, and the latter an aesthetic, expressive approach. The term *ch'ing* was, as Chu remarked, preferred over the term *chih* in the critical writings of Six Dynasties authors. See Chu Tzu-ch'ing, pp. 193–234. For an explication of the two terms (*chih* and *ch'ing*) and also *ching* (scene) in English see Owen, *Readings*, pp. 585–86.

14. Kuo and Wang, I, p. 61. *Notes on Music* is included in *The Book of Rites* (*Li-*

chi). Shen Yüeh, the poet of the Southern Dynasties, maintained that it was the work of Kung-sun Ni-tzu, a Confucian of the early Warring States period, around the late fifth century and the fourth century B.C. It was without doubt a work before the first century B.C.

15. Liu Hsi-tsai, *Yi-kai* (1927, reprint, Taipei: Kuang-wen shu-chü, 1964), *chüan* 2: *Shih-kai*, p. 18a. Hsieh An (320–85), aristocrat and Prime Minister of the Eastern Chin dynasty, once asked the youngsters of his family at a party to cite what each of them considered to be the best lines from the *Shih-ching*. His nephew Hsieh Hsüan (343–88) cited this stanza from *Ts'ai wei* as his choice. See *Shih-shuo hsin-yü chiao-chien*, I (IV, 52), p. 128.

16. See Chang Shao-k'ang, p. 1, and also Note 5, pp. 4–7. Chang cites copiously from Ch'ien Chung-shu's *Kuan chui p'ien*, III, p. 1177. *Yi* is a highly complicated term. See Chang's citation of Kuo Shao-yü's discussion on the term. For an English explication of the term see Owen, *Readings*, p. 594.

17. See Chang Shao-k'ang, p. 14, and also Note 4, pp. 17–18. Citing Ch'ien Chung-shu's remark (*Kuan chui p'ien*, III, p. 1182), Chang argues that Lu Chi emphasizes the things in nature in his concept of the *wu* but neglects things of a social nature.

18. See Chou Chen-fu ed., *Wen-hsin tiao-lung chu-shih*, XLVI, p. 493. All further citations from the *Wen-hsin tiao-lung*, with the number of the chapter and the pagination in parentheses in the text, are from this version. Stephen Owen has included this chapter in his selected translation of Liu Hsieh's book, and rendered the title of the chapter as "The Sensuous Colors of Physical Things," see his *Readings*, pp. 277–86.

19. Kōzen Hiroshi, "Wen-hsin tiao-lung te tzu-jan-kuan: t'an-pen so-yüan" ("The View of Nature in the *Wen-hsin tiao-lung*: Its Origins and Sources") in Wang Yüan-hua ed. *Jih-pen yen-chiu Wen-hsin tiao-lung lun-wen-chi* (Chi-nan: Ch'i-Lu shu-she, 1983), pp. 191–216.

20. See Owen, *Readings*, pp. 262–63. I am indebted to Professor Owen's suggestion for an English rendition of the term *han-hsü*. The term was used by the late T'ang poet Ssu-k'ung T'u (837–908) as one of his *Twenty-Four Categories of Poetry*, which found a new translation with extensive critical notes in Owen's book, see *Readings*, pp. 299–357; for the section on *han-hsü* see pp. 326–29.

21. The reader is invited to compare my translation with Owen's, who found the last line as cited here dubious in meaning in original. See *Readings*, p. 271 and p. 617, Note 204.

22. Kuo and Wang, I, p. 308.

23. Wang Li-ch'i, pp. 131–32. These are the fifteenth and the sixteenth *positions*.

24. Ou-yang Hsiu, *Liu-yi shih-hua*, from *Li-tai shih-hua*, pp. 264–72. This citation and the subsequent dialogue are on p. 267. The couplets that Mei Yao-ch'en used were from pentasyllabic regulated poems respectively by the T'ang poets Yen Wei (*In Response to Supernumerary Liu's Poem Sent to Me by Mail*, VIII, 2914); Wen T'ing-yün (*An Early Morning Trip in Mt. Shang-shan*, XVII, 6741); and Chia Tao (*Passing by a Mountain Village*, XVII, 6671).

25. Fan Hsi-wen, *Tui-ch'uang yeh-yü*, *chüan* 2, p. 2b. From Ting Fu-pao ed., *Li-tai shih-hua hsü-pien* (Taipei: Yi-wen ch'u-pan-she, 5 Vols., undated), II.

26. See Hsieh Chen, *Ssu-ming shih-hua*, in particular *chüan* 4, in Ting Fu-pao, IV. Wang Fu-chih, *Shih-yi* and *Hsi-t'ang yung-ji hsü-lun* (*Nei p'ien*), from Tai Hung-sen ed.,

Chiang-chai shih-hua chien-chu (Peking: Jen-min wen-hsüeh ch'u-pan-she, 1981), p. 33, p. 72. See also James J.Y. Liu, *Chinese Theories of Literature* (Chicago: University of Chicago Press, 1975), pp. 40–43. Stephen Owen has included selections from Wang Fu-chih's criticism in his *Readings*, see pp. 451–91.

27. Ch'i Chi, *Feng-shao chih-ko*, 8. From *Li-tai shih-hua hsü-pien*, I.

28. Hsü Yin, *Ya-tao chi-yao*. Cited from Wang Ta-p'eng ed., *Chung-kuo li-tai shih-hua hsüan*, I, p. 109.

29. Wen Yü, *Shih-ko*, from Wang Ta-p'eng, I, p. 132.

30. I have come upon discussions on the ending of Tu Fu's *Song of Fowls-trussing* in the following Sung sources: 1) Chang Piao-ch'eng, *Shan-hu-kou shih-hua*, in *Li-tai shi-hua*, I, p. 464. (Chang was citing the comments of the Sung poet Ch'en Shih-tao); 2) Fan Kung-ch'eng, *Kuo-t'ing lu*, in Hua Wen-hsüan ed. *Ku-tien wen-hsüeh yen-chiu chih-liao hui-pien: Tu Fu chüan*, II, p. 399; 3) Ch'en Chang-fang, *Pu-li k'o-tan*, in both Hua Wen-hsüan, II, p. 457; and Wang Ta-p'eng, II, p. 595; 4) Hung Mai, *Jung-chai sui-pi, chüan* 5, in Hua Wen-hsüan, II, p. 507; 5) Chao Tz'u-kung (Chao Yen-ts'ai), *Tu-shih hsiang-chu*, in Hua Wen-hsüan, II, p. 608; 6) Tseng Feng, *Chang Ts'an-chün chu-yi-ko chi*, in *Lü-tu chi*, *chüan* 19, Hua Wen-hsüan, III, p. 708; 7) Wang Mao, *Yeh-k'o ts'ung-shu, chüan* 25, cited in both Hua Wen-hsüan, III, p. 749 and Wang Ta-p'eng, II, p. 774; 8) Yü Wen-pao, *Ch'ui-chien san-lu*, Hua Wen-hsüan, III, p. 865.

31. Chiang K'uei, *Pai-shih Tao-jen shih-shuo*, from *Li-tai shih-hua*, II, pp. 679–83. For a learned and perceptive study of Chiang K'uei's theory and practice see Shuen-fu Lin, *The Transformation of the Chinese Lyrical Tradition: Chiang K'uei and Southern Sung Tz'u Poetry* (Princeton: Princeton University Press, 1978). See also James J.Y. Liu, "Chiang K'uei's Poetics," in Stephen C. Soong ed., *A Brotherhood in Song: Chinese Poetry and Poetics* (Hong Kong: The Chinese University Press, 1985), pp. 93–98.

32. Shen Yi-fu, *Yüeh-fu chih-mi*, from T'ang Kuei-chang ed., *Tz'u-hua ts'ung-pien* (1934, reprint, Hong Kong: Kuang-wen shu-chü, 12 Vols., 1967), I, pp. 229–47. This citation is from pp. 230–31.

33. See Chou Tzu-chih, *Chu-p'o shih-hua*, in *Li-tai shih-hua*, I, p. 341. The lines from Ho Chu's lyric-song are cited from the text in T'ang Kuei-chang ed. *Ch'üan Sung tz'u* (Shanghai: Chung-hua shu-chü, 5 Vols., 1965), I, p. 513.

34. The use of scenic closure as a conscious device is illustrated by the above-cited observations of Chiang K'uei and Shen Yi-fu, but a more comprehensive exploration of closure in the *tz'u* form has yet to be made.

35. The term *tuan chü* had been used in the Southern Dynasties period to refer to the quatrain, which was later supplanted by the term *chüeh chü* or "truncated lines."

36. Su Shih's comments on the poem were cited in Huei Hung's *Leng-chai yeh-hua*. Liu Ch'en-weng's rebuke of Su Shih's idea was cited in Chou T'ing's *T'ang-shih hsüan-mu hui-t'ung*. The other comments were respectively from Yen Yü's *Ts'ang-lang shih-hua*, Li Tung-yang's *Huai-lu-t'ang shih-hua*, Wang Shih-chen's (Ming) *Yi-yüan chih-yen* (*chüan* 4), Hu Ying-ling's *Shih-shou* (*Nei p'ien, chüan* 6), Wang Shih-chen's (Ch'ing) *Tai-ching-t'ang shih-hua*. See Ting Hsiu-hui, *Liu Ho-tung chi pien-nien chi-shih*, pp. 262–63. See also *T'ang-shih chien-shang tz'u-tien*, pp. 933–34. For the idiom see Chapter 1, note 8.

37. Stephen Owen, "Some Mid-T'ang Quatrains," in Soong, *A Brotherhood in Song*, pp. 145–78. This citation is from p. 147.

38. See Yu-kung Kao and Tsu-lin Mei, "Ending Lines in Wang Shih-chen's 'Ch'i-Chüeh': Convention and Creativity in the Ch'ing," in Christian F. Murck ed. *Artists and Traditions* (Princeton: Princeton University Press, 1976), pp. 131–44. The essay concentrates on the devices as used in the quatrain form of Wang Shih-chen.

39. *Chuangtzu*, from the chapter of *T'ien tao* (*The Heavenly Way*). Cited from Kuo and Wang, I, pp. 43–44.

40. *Lü-shih ch'un-ch'iu*, from the chapter of *Pen wei* (*The Essence of Flavor*).

41. Yen Yü, *Ts'ang-lang shih-hua*, cited from Kuo and Wang, II, p. 424. For an English translation of the work, with critical notes, see Owen, *Readings*, pp. 391–420.

42. See Ch'en Chang-fang's *Pu-li k'o-t'an*, cited in Wang Ta-p'eng, II, p. 595; Wang Mao's *Yeh-k'o ts'ung-shu* (*chüan* 25) in Wang Ta-p'eng, II, p. 774; Yü Wen-pao's *Ch'ui-chien san-lu* in Wang Ta-p'eng, II, p. 903; Wei Liao-weng's *Hou shih Shao-ling shih-chu hsü*, in his *Ho-shan hsien-sheng ta-ch'üan-chi* (*chüan* 55), cited in Hua Wen-hsüan, III, p. 804; Chen Te-hsiu's *Wen-chang cheng-tsung*, cited in Hua Wen-hsüan, III, p. 976.

43. Cited in Chou Chen-fu, *Shih-tz'u li-hua* (Peking: Chung-kuo ch'ing-nien ch'u-pan-she, Second Edition, 1979), p. 392.

6

An Open Ending: Towards the Western Horizon

WHILE poetic closure was a perennially discussed subject as an integral part of poetic structure in Chinese literary criticism, it had been largely overlooked as such in the West until the late 1960's, when Barbara Herrnstein Smith's pioneering study of the topic was published. As she mentioned in the preface of the book, although literary theorists since Aristotle have been occupied with beginnings, middles, and ends, there had not been any serious treatment of poetic closure as a subject in its own right.[1] The texts discussed in *Poetic Closure* are primarily restricted to English and American poems, with an acknowledged bias for those of sixteenth and seventeenth centuries; but Smith maintained that few poems in other languages and periods ("classical, medieval, continental, or non-European poetry") would be found to have structural or closural features that utterly elude the classifications offered in the book (ix). She also claimed to have assumed in the book "a universal psychology of closure," which she believed to be justified by her reading of translations from non-European poetry. Hence, Smith maintained that what she said of poetic closure would, hopefully, be "as true of Hopi and Hindustani as it seems to be of English, Latin, German, French, Italian, and Spanish poetry" (Note 28, 32–33).

Smith's study has many and various merits, in particular it has opened a new horizon for the reading of poetry. Some problems arise, however, when we attempt to place the scenic closure of Chinese poetry in a comparative perspective. As previously discussed, since the age of the High T'ang such ending was employed in Chinese poetry and recognized in poetics. The scenic closure found its aesthetic ground in the necessity and beauty of incompleteness, in the artistic search for "unending meanings," and in a suspicion of language itself as an efficient vehicle for the expression and communication of complex human feelings and thoughts. Such aesthetic contexts and values would place Chinese scenic closure very close to what Smith has chosen to call *anti-closure*, a type of ending which avoids "the expressive qualities of strong closure while securing, in various ways, the reader's sense of the poem's integrity" (242). Smith, however, has changed from an a-historical to a historical approach over this issue, and identified the *anti-closure* with modern poetry only, which is probably justifiable in the case of Western poetry. In fact, the only text discussed in the book that has an ending approximate to the Chinese scenic closure, particularly to that of a poem like Tu Fu's *Song of Fowls-Trussing*, is Robert Lowell's poem, *The Drinker*. Smith has cited the poem as one of her examples for the tendency in modern poetry which, according to her, refuses to make final comments and to draw conclusions (252–253).

Smith has also suggested in her discussion that the tendency towards anti-closure is a part of the "stylistic multiplicity" of modern times, "when almost every poetic tradition that has ever existed—native or foreign, Western or Oriental, classical or medieval—is to some extent viable" (235). She has not, however, identified any particular tradition as having exerted an influence on this tendency in Western poetry.

It should be noted here that despite the close encounter between East and West cultures in modern times, and the ever increasing knowledge of and influence on each other, there is still some basic difference, in addition to spatial and temporal incompatibility, between the concept of closure in Chinese poetry, especially that represented by the scenic closure since the High T'ang, and the concept of *anti-closure* in modern Western poetry.

To fully understand the differences between the two traditions, it is necessary to examine, as a first step, samples of Western poetry before it could possibly have received any direct influence or inspiration from Chinese poetry and poetics. Was the scenic closure ever used then? If so, in what capacity or variety? Did its use ever become a kind of fashion or convention? And finally, did it ever become a part of Western critical consciousness, as it did in the Chinese context?

Scenic closure, though unmentioned in Smith's book, and indeed, not widely adopted as it has been in Chinese poetry, may still be found in pre-modern Western poetry. A few Western poems from different periods and traditions are singled out in what follows, with an emphasis on their endings in image. The first of these is the sixteenth poem from *Les Regrets* (1558), the sonnet sequence by the French Renaissance poet Joachim Du Bellay:

Ce pendant que Magny suit son grand Avanson,
Panjas son Cardinal, et moy le mien encore,
Et que l'espoir flateur, qui noz beaux ans devore,
Appaste noz desirs d'un friand hamesson,

Tu courtises les Roys et d'un plus heureaux son
Chantant l'heur de Henry, qui son siecle decore,
Tu t'honores toymesme, et celuy qui honore
L'honneur que tu luy fais par ta docte chanson.

Las, et nous ce pendant nous consumons nostre aage
Sur le bord incogneu d'un estrange rivage,
Ou la malheur nous fait ces tristes vers chanter:

Comme on voit quelquefois, quand la mort les appelle,
Arrangez flanc à flanc parmy l'herbe nouvelle,
Bien loin sur un estang trois cygnes lamenter.[2]

[While Magny follows his great Avanson,
Panjas his cardinal, and I mine as well,
And while beguiling hope, devouring our heyday,
Entices our desires with a sapid bait.

You attend upon kings, and in a happier strain
Sing for the pleasure of Henry, who glorifies the age,
You win honor for yourself, and for him who honors
The honor that you bring him by your learned song,

While we, alas, consume our days
On the unknown brink of an alien seashore
Where sorrow makes us sing these sad lines,

As one sees sometimes, when death summons them,
Arrayed side by side among fresh grass,
Far, far across a pond, three swans lamenting.]

This sonnet sequence was about the poet's experience while working in Italy as secretary to his uncle, the cardinal Jean Du Bellay, in the company of his two friends, the poet Olivier de Magny, and Jean de Panjas. This poem is the first of a series (16–22) addressed to the other leading poet of le Pléiade, his friend Pierre de Ronsard, who was staying in the French court at the time. However, the first person singular here, like that in the other poems of the sequence, is not to be taken literally to be the author himself. Rather, what is assumed here is the fictional voice of a homesick poet, expressing his envy of a more fortunate peer, who could enjoy all the glory and fame back in France; all the while, the former is using this admiration as a pretext for a poetic competition with the latter.[3] The thematic messages of the poem are in fact close to some of the standard themes of classical Chinese poetry: aspiration for fame and honor, and the complaint about wasting one's talent in an unbecoming environment.

The poem, written in alexandrines, reveals a kind of internal symmetry between its two quatrains and between the two tercets: the former form a contrastive pair, and the latter a comparative pair. The first quatrain opens with an almost matter-of-fact account of the poet himself and his two friends, and then immediately places the trio in a setting which is to form a sharp contrast with that of the addressee in the next stanza. In the first quatrain, the three cardinals serve as foils to the speaker and his two friends, then in the second, the person serving the same function is Henry II, the French king, who is set as a foil for Ronsard, the latter being addressed in the familiar *tu*. The contrast between the setting of the three friends and that of Ronsard is not only signified by the use of deictic personal pronouns (*nous* versus *tu*), but also highlighted by the accompanying figures of the Roman *Cardinals* versus the French *Roy*. There is a play with the word *L'honneur* and its derivatives *honores* and *honore* in lines 7–8, accentuated by the *enjambement* as well as its use as the *rejet*, that increases and extends the resounding effect of the word group.

The interjection *Las* (shortened form for *hélas*) at the beginning of the first tercet resumes the tone of *Regret* of the first quatrain, and continues the contrast in the second, which is illustrated by the use of *la malheur* (line 11) versus *l'heur* (line 6), and *ces tristes vers* (line 11) against *plus heureaux son* (line 5). In giving a variation of the image of the trio in the first quatrain, it also provides the object for the simile which is to be presented in the second tercet.

The renowned French critic Sainte-Beuve praised the closing tercet highly as a great poetic conclusion.[4] In agreement with one of the principles that Du Bellay advocated in his literary manifesto, *La Deffence et Illustration de la Langue Françoise*, the very use of the swan image harks back to classical convention. In Plato's *Phaedo*, Socrates claimed before his execution that he had in himself the spirit of prophecy like the swans: "For they, when they perceive that they must die, having sung all their life long, do then sing more than ever, rejoicing in the thought that they are about to go away to the god whose ministers they are."[5]

The identification of swans and poets probably derived from the Greek myth which always placed swans in the company of Apollo, god of music and fine arts. A Pythagorean fable says that the soul of all good poets pass into swans. Hence the epithet of Homer is the *Swan of Ionia*, Virgil the *Swan of Mantua*, and Shakespeare the *Swan of Avon*.[6]

It has been suggested that the source of this poetic image is in Virgil's *Aeneid*.[7] But Du Bellay's transposition is an ingenious structural device that moves far beyond simple borrowing. By placing an extended simile of this kind, which probably derived from the epic tradition, at the very end of the poem, he has created an image that appeals to the reader's inward eye, leading it *bien loin* in the distance, an avian *tableau vivant* that illuminates the central theme of the entire text, as laid out in the statement of the three stanzas preceding this final tercet. Also, the sad state of the dying swans is intensified by having them placed among *l'herbe nouvelle*, a juxtaposition suggestive of the sharp contrast of life versus death. Besides the figurative nature of the tercet, its language, in contrast to the pomp wordplay of previous lines, becomes more direct, simple and yet highly lyrical, with its tempo slowed down by the use of alliteration and assonance, adding to the lingering visual effect of the image.

True to his advocacy of learning from Greek and Latin models, Du Bellay adopted in his sonnets not only the theme of the classical *elegy* (used in the sense of a love plaint by Ovid), but even the very form of the closing simile, a measure employed in classical poetry. The Roman poet Catullus, for example, used it on several occasions. In one of the poems (No. 11) in the so-called "Lesbia Cycle," the speaker asks the messengers sent him by Lesbia, the woman he once loved, to take a message back. It concludes thus (ll. 21–24):

> nec meum respectet, ut aute, amorem,
> qui illius culpa cecidit uelut prati
> ultimi flos, praetereunte postquam
> tactus aratro est.
>
> [She is not to expect my love, as she used to,
> For through her fault it has dropped
> Like a flower, at the edge of the field,
> Touched by the passing plough.]

In another, a satiric occasional poem (No. 25), the speaker chides and threatens someone who has stolen from him some personal belongings, demanding that these be returned at once. Here Catullus again employs a figurative ending (ll. 10–13):

ne laneum latusculum manusque mollicellas
inusta turpiter tibi flagella conscribillent,
et insolenter aestues, uelut minuta magno
deprensa nauis in mari, uesaniente uento.[8]

[Or you'll find your soft flanks and delicate hands
Scribbled all over shamefully by a lash
And you'll toss around as never before, as a little boat
Caught in a raging windstorm.]

These image endings possess the closural element that Smith has referred to as the thematic device of *closural allusion* (172–182). The three swans in Du Bellay's sonnet, besides bringing the central image of the speaker himself and his friends (poets as swans) to a state of consummation, are lamenting about the approaching death. The same is true of the two examples from Catullus—be it the image of a plough crushing the flower (fallen love), or the suggestion of a shipwreck (sinking boat). However, being more visual than cerebral, such closure heightens and intensifies the rhetorical and thematic effects of the whole text, inviting the reader to further extend his imagination. It is close in spirit to the ending of a poem like Tu Fu's *Night Thoughts on a Voyage* in finding a different way of closing the text through non-statement.

A different type of scenic closure is found in the famous short poem *Hälfte des Lebens* (*Middle Age*) by Friedrich Hölderlin:

Mit gelben Birnen hänget
Und voll mit wilden Rosen
Das land in den See,
Ihr holden Schwäne,
Und trunken von Küssen
Tunkt ihr das Haupt
Ins heilignüchterne Wasser.

Weh mir, wo nehm ich, wenn
Es Winter ist, die Blumen, und wo
Den Sonnenschein
Und Schatten der Erde?
Die Mauern stehn
Sprachlos und kalt, im Winde
Klirren die Fahnen.[9]

[With yellow pears hangs
    and full of wild roses
    the land down into the lake,
You lovely swans,
    and drunk with kisses
    you dip your heads
    into the sacredly sober water.

Woe is me! where shall I get, when
    it's winter, flowers? and where
    the sunshine
    and the shade of earth?
The walls stand
    speechless and cold, in the wind
    rattle the flags.]

This was one of the last poems that Hölderlin saw into print before he sank entirely into the silence of insanity. The choice of diction in the first stanza is in general that of common speech, with one exception in the collocation of the coined adjective *heilignüchterne* and the noun *Wasser*; but the syntax is disjointed and reversed, most likely in a deliberate way. In a full display of poetic license, the word *hänget* has been shifted from its normal position, which would be either at the beginning or the end of line 3, to the end of the first; the conjunction *Und*, which ordinarily should make more sense if placed at the beginning of line 4, is now placed at the beginning of the next line. Such unusual manipulation of word and syntax helps to defamiliarize and intensify the images, ad to create a tension throughout the entire text. The predominant use of *enjambement* helps to achieve a staccato effect that agrees with the paratactic organization and the hesitant tone of the poem.

The first stanza presents two separate images that apparently have no connection with each other: that of the land that hangs, heavy with yellow pears and wild roses, down into the lake, and that of the swans dipping their heads into the water. The two images nevertheless fuse into one harmonious scene of lushness and serenity. The image of the swans, in its association with the soul of poets in the classical convention, may allude to the autobiographical nature of the poem, which is somewhat signified in the title, though hardly made explicit in the text.

At the beginning of the second stanza there is a sudden outburst of emotion which comes quite unexpectedly, forming a sharp turn from the serene scene preceding it. The image of the grim winter looms large over all previous happy images, even though traces of those (*die Blumen, Den Sonnenschein*) still exist (in their absence, though, as the question bespeaks) in the lines. This outburst takes the form of a question, which is being lengthened by the use of commas and *enjambement*. It is a question that is left unanswered at the end; what follows instead is again a pair of images that likewise have no obvious connection with each other, only this time these are not images of nature, but rather of cultural makings. The animation of inanimate things (walls standing silent and cold, flags rattling in the wind) in the last three lines is highly symbolic: the word *Mauern* connotes barrier, obstacle, enclosure, isolation. One is led to ask: who is, or what are, *sprachlos und kalt*? the speaker? or the walls? Is it a kind of empathy (*Einfülung*) felt by the speaker of the poem? The image here is both auditory and visual. Silence and sound act together, with the latter (the rattling of the flags) further enhancing the former.

The sharp contrast between the images of the two stanzas sheds some light on the title, which probably refers to the poet's own age at the time of composition, which was about the midpoint of the conventional human life span (threescore and ten). Was he seeing his first half (*Hälfte*) of life like the serene summer scene as in the first strophe, but trembling at the gloomy latter half as one of darkness and depression? The word *sprachlos* does seem to forecast the silence that the poet sank into shortly after this poem was written. Or was the poet talking about life in a more universal sense, seeing humankind at the crossroads, between the age of faith that he saw as fading out, and the incoming era of chaos where, to use Matthew Arnold's metaphor in his *Dover Beach*, "ignorant armies clash by night"? Whatever the meaning is, this is a poem that, in the words of Martin Heidegger (who called Hölderlin the *poet of the poet*), "invents its world of images and remains immersed in the realm of the imagined."[10] Furthermore, the highly symbolic nature of the images makes this poem a precedent for the transition from a poetry of statement to a poetry of suggestion in the middle of the nineteenth century, with the practice of Baudelaire and the French Symbolists, and from there further on to Ezra Pound and the American Imagists. It was no accident that the re-discovery of Hölderlin, promoted by poets like Stefan George, occurred simultaneously with an embrace of Mallarmé and the Symbolist poetics in the West.[11]

The poem with an ending in image that seems to best parallel the suggestive aesthetics of its Chinese equivalents is one by Shelley, the

English Romantic poet who, in the words of Douglas Bush, became "the whipping-boy of modern criticism,"[12] and whose poetics seems often to be in direct conflict with that of most twentieth-century poets:

Ozymandias

I met a traveller from an antique land
Who said: Two vast and trunkless legs of stone
Stand in the desert...Near them, on the sand,
Half sunk, a shattered visage lies, whose frown,
And wrinkled lip, and sneer of cold command,
Tell that its sculptor well those passions read
Which yet survive, stamped on these lifeless things,
The hand that mocked them and the heart that fed:
And on the pedestal these words appear:
"My name is Ozymandias, king of kings:
Look on my works, ye Mighty, and despair!"
Nothing beside remains. Round the decay
Of that colossal wreck, boundless and bare
The lone and level sands stretch far away.[13]

Harold Bloom once argued, not without justification, that of all Romantic poets Shelley needed the closest reading, and that it ought to be a reading with its context in the traditions of poetry, not those of philosophy or politics.[14] It may still be the case at present, though in the case of *Ozymandias*, a close reading of the poem can hardly exclude its philosophical and political aspects.

Such a reading may well start from the title itself. *Ozymandias* is the Greek translation of the Egyptian name, *User-Ma'at-Ra*, of Rameses II, the ancient Egyptian monarch of the 13th century B.C., who had commissioned the carving of a great number of gigantic statues of himself. The word *Ozymandias*, the *Greek* name of an *Egyptian* pharaoh, carries in itself a hybrid sense of both familiarity and quaintness: no better name could be used as a synonym for all kinds of repressive dictatorships that the poet abhorred.

There was an earlier draft of the poem, which has survived, in its unfinished fragmentary form, as follows:

There stands by Nile a single pedestal,
On which two trunkless legs of crumbling stone.
Quiver through sultry mist; beneath the sand
Half sunk a shattered visage lies, whose frown

And wrinkled lips impatient of command
Betray some sculptor's art, who...[15]

Instead of the simple third person narrative frame of this earlier draft, a much more complex framework has been introduced in the final version: there are several different levels of voice in the poem. First of all, there is the first person singular *I*, the speaker who starts the poem. His role of narration is immediately taken over in line 2 by a second narrator, the *traveller from an antique land*. Both he and the land he comes from are preceded by indefinite articles, which convey a sense of vagueness and generality. From the second line onwards through the end, the poem becomes the speech of this traveller. There is an interlude in lines 10–11 which, as an inscription on the pedestal of the statue, assumes a third voice, that of the invisible Ozymandias (seen only in the synecdochic remnants of his statue). Behind all this arrangement, of course, there is the underlying voice of Shelley himself, the "unacknowledged legislator of the world" in his role as a poet.

Besides the complex narrative framework, the temporal and spatial dimensions of the poem are also multi-leveled, as a result of what we may call the *poetic gambit* that Shelley chose over the earlier version. The very first line introduces two levels of the preterit: first, a recent one as signified by the past tense verb *met*, and second, a remote one indicated by the adjective *antique*. The absence of the immediacy of the present tense (*now*), frequently found in lyric poems, seems to provide a temporal distance between the occasion (of the meeting) and the present time (both the *present* of the author's composition, and the *present* of the reader's reading act). There is also a suggestion of spatial polarization in the noun *traveller* and the preposition *from*, though it is not explicitly stated by any deictic terms. The spatial *other* is represented by the word *desert*, which finds a variation in the word *sands* in the last line. After the first line, the scene immediately comes to a close view of the statue in the traveller's narration. In the last three lines, however, there is a sudden shift from the close look of the remnants of the statue in the foreground, to a distant look to the background, thus expanding the poetic space and leading the reader's imaginary eye, as well as that of the first speaker, presumably, all the way across the desert to the far horizon.

To those who have often complained that Shelley was incapable of effective reasoning and intellectual control of his emotional outpourings, this poem may have seemed atypical in his *oeuvre*.[16] Everything in this poem is implicit, controlled, even subdued. Structurally, the poem is in the form of an Italian sonnet which consists of an octave and a sestet, though these are not visibly separated on the page. Its rhyme scheme (*abab / acdc / ede / fef*) defies standard classifications, although it is not as careless as it has been considered by many to be. Its pattern is like that of a chain of rings: one rhyme from each of the unmarked structural units recurs in the next. Such an interweaving texture helps to increase the sense of consistency and compactness of the entire text.

The poem does nevertheless reveal the structural format of its Italian prototype. The break between the two parts is accentuated by the use of the conjunction *And* at the beginning of line 9. Following the Petrarchan convention, the sestet is further divided into two tercets. The first tercet is the only place in the poem where those *passions* (line 6) become apparent in the form of speech, actually a speech-in-speech, supposedly in the ancient pharaoh's own words. Its pomp and arrogance are deliberately set for contrast with the seemingly cool, noncommittal tone of the final tercet which, instead of making any explicit comments, chooses to return to the apparently indifferent descriptive mode as in the octave. Only this time, as mentioned above, it shifts the reader's inner eye from the proximate vision to the distant vision. The caesura in line 12, made obvious by the use of the period, provides a pause for meditation before it moves on again to the distance. The choice of two pairs of alliterative words with alternative long and short vowels (*boundless and bare / lone and level*) helps to decelerate the pace towards the end, creating a resounding echo, and enhancing the lingering flavor of the ending.

The non-statement ending, forming a sharp contrast to the bombastic message as conveyed in the inscription interlude, is a silent image of emptiness that, in the Chinese poet Tu Fu's words, "joins the vast." It is exactly this ending that works the text to its climax, with all its implication and irony left for the reflection of the reader.

In terms of poetic tradition, Shelley is following in the wake of Milton in employing the sonnet as what Wordsworth called a "trumpet," a measure for political commentary (for example, in Shelley's *On the Late Massacre in Piedmont*). With all its artistic beauty and implicitness, *Ozymandias* is primarily a political satire against monarchs and kings (whom Shelley regarded as anachronisms in his age), and implicitly against all kinds of repressive authority. The political message comes out more clearly if it is compared with a later poem, *England in 1819*:

An old, mad, blind, despised, and dying king—
Princes, the dregs of their dull race, who flow
Through public scorn—mud from a muddy spring;
Rulers who neither see, nor feel, nor know,
But leechlike to their fainting country cling,
Till they drop, blind in blood, without a blow;...

This is not a weak poem. Structured in a paratactic order of enumeration, it is a forceful accusation of the British monarchy in its many phases. Yet, compared to *Ozymandias*, the message lies mostly on the surface, and there is not much inner depth for the reader to explore and muse upon.

The Chinese critic Hung Mai compared Tu Fu's *Song of Fowls-trussing* with a later poem, Li Te-yüan's *Song of Boats East and West*, in order to show the artistic superiority of the former. Likewise, *Ozymandias* has been placed alongside a poem by Arthur Guiterman, an American humorist, as a topic for discussion:

On the Vanity of Earthly Greatness

The tusks that clashed in mighty brawls
Of mastodons, are billiard balls.
The sword of Charlemagne the Just
Is ferric oxide, known as rust.

The grizzly bear whose potent hug
Was feared by all, is now a rug.
Great Caesar's bust is on the shelf,
And I don't feel so well myself.[17]

I. A. Richards once observed that it would often be more difficult to identify bad poetry than good poetry.[18] In the present case, the problem lies in the fact that the two poems belong to different poetic sub-genres, with different expectations from the reader. As a sample of light verse, Guiterman's poem may well be considered to have achieved its own aim: a hearty chuckle at the *bathos* created by the seemingly absurd yet "scientific" juxtaposition of images. However, it certainly lacks the *magnitude* or *high seriousness* that one may find in *Ozymandias*, which are the *touchstones* for great art, as critics from Aristotle to Matthew Arnold have suggested. If we may place Shelley's text in the perspective of Chinese literary criticism, then the excellence of *Ozymandias* lies precisely in its implicitness and suggestiveness, in its "meaning beyond words" (*yen wai chih yi*), much of which has been created by the use of its scenic closure, a closure that makes its comment through the absence of commentary.

From the examples of three poets of different historical periods and poetic conventions, we see that scenic closure actually had been used well before the fusion of intercultural ideas in modern age in the West, for various effects. In all these poems, their endings in image further enrich the text: some with classical allusions, some with symbolic message, and some with ironical suggestions. Such examples, however, were indeed exceptions, even among the works of these poets, as well as in pre-modern Western poetry in general. Moreover, there has been little, if any, critical attention directed toward the use of scenic closure, despite the fact that all three poems are among the most anthologized texts, through the vicissitudes of canonization, of their respective authors.[19] Does the phenomenon, then, suggest any essential difference between Chinese and Western poetry and poetics? Is there really "a universal psychology of closure" as Barbara Herrnstein Smith has assumed?

To better investigate into these questions, it may be illuminating, it seems to me, to look into the early reception of Chinese poetry in the West, *early* enough, for example, to have preceded the demand in the West for poetic innovation in this century, which so often looked to "the Oriental" for new sources of inspiration.

Since the days of Marco Polo China had loomed as a large and exotic presence on the European cultural horizon; but, for a long period in the last few centuries, Chinese poetry did not make as much impression on Westerners as Chinese philosophy and ethics, which attracted such prominent thinkers like Leibniz and Spinoza, or even as Chinese fiction and drama, which could rank among its early admirers such distinguished writers as Voltaire and Goethe.[20] David Hawkes has observed that the study of Chinese poetry in the West lagged far behind the study of Chinese philosophy, and that although a few translations from Chinese verse appeared from time to time, there was nothing which could have conceivably interested a Western poet until the publication of the *Livre de jade* (1867), a collection of Chinese poems translated into French by Judith Walter, the daughter of Théophile Gautier.[21]

This translation, and to a lesser extent the earlier French translation, *Poésis de l'époque des Thang* (1842) by the sinologist Marquis d'Hervey-Saint-Denys, gave poetry a place, insignificant as it was, in the growing *chinoiserie*. Judith Walter's translation received a laudatory review from the poet Verlaine, for example, who compared it to Aloysius Bertrand's *Gaspard de la nuit*. Verlaine observed that, if he were to choose between the two, he would prefer *Livre de jade* "pour son originalité plus grande, sa forme plus pure, sa poésie plus réelle et plus intense" ["for its greater originality, its more perfect form, its more genuine and intense poetic quality"].[22] Other than eliciting this singular, vague remark of Verlaine's, however, the influence of Chinese poetry on the changing Western (particularly French) poetics of the age seemed to be very limited. It only became more substantial when it spread into the English-speaking world, along with the works of Baudelaire, Mallarmé, and the Symbolist poetics, at the turn of the century.[23]

Through most of the nineteenth century, Western reception of Chinese poetry, aside from being a display of curiosity, was in general not so favorable. As Mary Gertrude Mason has remarked, "Europeans admired Chinese poetry but felt that something was lacking." She also noted that a reader of Hervey-Saint-Denys's translation made the comment that Chinese poems conveyed nothing of a superior world or Supreme Being, and they lacked depth and perspective because they were imbued with no great religious doctrine.[24] As late as 1875, W. H. Medhurst, a diplomat and scholar, asserted in a lecture he gave in Shanghai that Chinese poetry, as a result of its rigid prosody and metrical construction, was "but a cramped and stunted representative of the sister art in other countries." He further observed:

> My reading of Chinese poetry, I must confess, has been but limited, but judging from analogy, which one may safely do with a people of stereotyped ideas like the Chinese, I think I can confidently assert that the Chinese poem has yet to be found which will bear perusal from beginning to end with the sustained interest that enchains the attention when reading any of the many European or American compositions which are familiar to all our minds.

After making such generalization on the basis of his self-acknowledged "limited" reading, Medhurst declared, with no less stout confidence: "As regards translations, there can be little hope of their ever becoming a vehicle for presenting Chinese poetry in an effective form to the foreign reader."[25] It may be interesting for us to notice the time when this gentleman, who showed in this lecture an unusual narrow-mindedness towards the Chinese people and Chinese civilization in general, was delivering it, presumably to an audience that consisted of other European diplomats and tourists. An interesting note here: it was only four decades before the publication of Ezra Pound's *Cathay*.

Actually the world did not have to wait for Pound to disprove such prejudice as Medhurst displayed. Before the century was over, Herbert A. Giles, who had just come back from China and taken up the tenure of professorship of Chinese at Oxford University, published his *Chinese Poetry in English Verse* in London. This was the book that, in the words of another sinologist, V. W. W. S. Purcell, "first rescued Chinese verse for English literature."[26] According to a study of the topic by Roy Earl Teele, Giles's was the first translation of Chinese poetry which not only reached sinologists, but also literary men and the public.[27]

There are many reasons why this book enjoyed success in the *fin-de-siècle* years of the nineteenth century, a transitional stage in the history of European literature. First of all, Giles excelled most previous Western translators of Chinese poetry in one aspect: he was a man of refined literary taste, conversant with the Western literary heritage.[28] His father was a classical scholar, and his own first book was on Cicero and Longinus. He was also quite competent in versifying, and well equipped with an armory of Victorian poetic diction. Even Arthur Waley, who usually preferred to adopt free verse over rhyme, and who once exchanged bitter notes with Giles over issues of translation, felt obliged to admit that the latter's translation "combines rhyme and literalness with wonderful dexterity."[29]

As a man of letters himself, a quality which, unfortunately, was (and perhaps still is) rare among sinologists, Giles was among the first to perceive some of the essential features of Chinese poetry which marked it as different from its Western counterpart. In *A History of Chinese Literature*, another *tour de force* published in 1901, Giles, made the following observation when he discussed the T'ang dynasty, the age that in his words produced "the best efforts" in poetry:

> A long poem does not appeal to the Chinese mind. ... Brevity is indeed the soul of a Chinese poem, which is valued not so much for what it says as for what it suggests. As in painting, so in poetry suggestion is the end and aim of the artist, who in each case may be styled an impressionist. The ideal length is twelve lines, and this is the limit set to candidates at the great public examinations at the present day, the Chinese holding that if a poet cannot say within such compass what he has to say it may very well be left unsaid. The eight-line poem is also a favourite, and so, but for its extreme difficulty, is the four-line epigram, or "stop-short," so called because of its abruptness, though, as the critics explain, "it is only the words which stop, the sense goes on," some train of thought having been

suggested to the reader ... The third line is considered the most troublesome to produce, some poets even writing it first; the last line should contain a "surprise" or *dénouement*.[30] We are, in fact, reminded of the old formula, "Omne epigramma sit instar apis," &c., better known in its English dress:—

"The qualities rare in a bee that we meet
in an epigram never should fail;
The body should always be little and sweet,
And a sting should be left in the tail."[31]

Giles may have exaggerated the importance of the shorter forms, as the T'ang dynasty was in fact also an age that resounded with the voices of Tu Fu, Han Yü, and Po Chü-yi in their great longer poems.[32] It was somewhat misleading, too, to identify the "unending sense" only with the Chinese quatrain (what Giles rendered as the *stop-shorts*). Nevertheless Giles did first reveal to the Western reader some important concepts in Chinese poetics, particularly in the poetics of the T'ang dynasty, such as the significance of suggestiveness and the demand for a forceful ending.

That Giles's anthology was more successful in its reception in the West than all its predecessors was also asserted in a review written in 1908 by Lytton Strachey, the well-known historian, biographer and critic. Strachey did not like contemporary poets like Yeats, who represented a new poetics at the time. But as a central figure in the avant-garde Bloomsbury group, Strachey played an important role in the changing critical stances at the beginning of the century; and in this essay he proved himself to be an important "person who understands the sound" (*chih yin*) in his perspicacious remarks on the similarities and differences between Chinese and Western poetry.[33]

From the very beginning of his review Strachey evaluated Giles's anthology not as translations, but rather as poetry in its own right, claiming that, although the book had been published ten years earlier, it contained the best poetry that his generation had known. He identified the spirit of Chinese poetry with the Western classical spirit, and then made an insightful observation upon the "curious contrast" between Chinese and Greek poetry:

Greek art is, in every sense of the word, the *most finished* in the world; it is for ever seeking to express what it has to express *completely* and *finally*; and when it has accomplished that, it is content. Thus the most exquisite of the lyrics in the Greek Anthology are, fundamentally, epigrams—though they are, of course, epigrams transfigured by passion and the highest splendours of art. One reads

> them, and one is filled, in a glorified and ethereal manner, with the same kind of satisfaction as that produced by a delicious mouthful of wine. One has had a draught of hippocrene, a taste of the *consummation* of beauty, and then one turns over the page, and pours out another glass. Different, indeed, is the effect of Chinese lyric. It is the very converse of the epigram; it aims at producing an impression which, so far from being final, must be *merely the prelude to a long series of visions and of feelings*. It hints at wonders; and the revelation which at last it gives us is *never a complete one*—it is clothed in the indefinability of our subtlest thoughts... "The words stop," say the Chinese, "but the sense goes on." The blind is drawn aside for a moment, and we catch a glimpse of a vision which starts us off on a mysterious voyage down the widening river of imagination.[34]

Reflecting upon this review, Arthur Waley accused Strachey, not without some justification, of having based his praise merely on a preference for certain limited forms of poetry.[35] To some extent Strachey suffered the same limitation as Giles: an emphasis *de trop* on the shorter forms of Chinese poetry. However, Strachey's observation penetrated into some of the basic differences between Chinese poetry and pre-modern Western poetry, particularly that regarding the Western concept of completeness, consummation and finality, versus the Chinese poetics of incompleteness and open-endedness.

Strachey's essay was published only two years before 1910, the year around which, according to Virginia Woolf's ironic observation, "human character changed," and with it came "a change in religion, conduct, politics, and literature."[36] The essay certainly played a role in further stimulating the interest in Chinese poetry among literary circles, and in popularizing it among the larger reading public. In the next two decades, translations of Chinese poetry mushroomed and prospered.[37] In addition, Strachey's essay also marked the beginning, on the eve of modernism, of a new, genuine appreciation of Chinese poetry and poetics, one that regarded them as essentially different from their Western counterparts, rather than submitting them to the criteria established in the West.

Besides the emphasis on suggestiveness and on the "unending sense," another possible difference between Chinese and Western poetry was noticed by Arthur Waley. In the introduction to the new edition (1962) of his little anthology, *A Hundred and Seventy Chinese Poems*, Waley commented on the great success of the book since its first publication in 1918:

> I think one of the reasons that it remained in fairly steady demand for forty years is that it appeals to people who do not ordinarily read poetry... The reason they

> got on all right with Chinese poetry was, I think, that it mainly deals with the concrete and particular, with things one can touch and see—a beautiful tree or lovely person—and not with abstract conceptions such as Beauty and Love. The English upper class, on the other hand, brought up at the universities in a tradition inspired largely by Plato, has reconciled itself to abstractions and even to the belief that the general is, in some mysterious way, truer and nobler than the particular. But ordinary people in England have very little use for abstractions and when poetry, under the influence of higher education, becomes abstract, it bores them.[38]

In a populist dry humor which may have come from his lifelong distaste for academia, Waley's observation disclosed some basic differences between the two traditions. Further on in the article, Waley noted that E. M. Forster, the famous novelist and writer, in reviewing one of Waley's books, had remarked that Chinese poems were *lovely* but *not beautiful*. Waley suggests that Forster was "expressing a demand for the ideal as opposed to the real." The view that something essential was lacking in Chinese poetry actually dated back to the early nineteenth century, as had been observed by Mary Gertrude Mason, cited earlier in the chapter.

Traditional Chinese poetry was not lacking in texts that invoked abstract principles, such as the poetry of Taoist discourse (*hsüan-yen shih*) popular during the fourth century. But the main current in Chinese aesthetics since the High T'ang, which found its expression, for example, in the words of Yen Yü (that poetry involves "a particular material that has nothing to do with books" and "a particular interest that has nothing to do with reason"), indeed celebrated the capacity to express the abstract and general through the concrete and particular, to fuse the external scene in the great cosmos with the internal world of human feelings and emotions. The use of the scenic closure in Chinese poetry since the High T'ang was precisely a deliberate maneuvering at the poet's hand that derived from such a poetics.

The aesthetics behind Chinese scenic closure, the poetics of incompleteness and suggestiveness, share some similarities with modernist Western poetics. However, the scenic closure is yet to be recognized as a conscious device in modern Western poetry, which places Smith's assumption of a universal psychology of closure into question. Purcell, in his discussion of the spirit of Chinese poetry, made the following remark which seems to be equally applicable to such an assumption:

> It is said that what are known as "universal ideas" are common to the world at large, and that these at least are susceptible of translation. But "universal" in this sense is really "European" and "idea" is unconsciously limited to the idea of Plato.[39]

Heidegger has also suggested, "Whatever is universal, that is to say, what is valid for many, can only be reached through a process of comparison."[40] To reach such "a universal psychology of poetic endings," then, one has to make comparisons on a more comprehensive scale, one that involves the close reading of poems of other cultures, not as odd pieces in translation, but rather in the context of each of their respective poetic traditions.

Western poetics has never entirely overlooked the significance of suggestiveness and incompleteness, just as Chinese poetry has never been entirely free from abstraction. As early as in the age of the ancient Greeks Theophrastus, Aristotle's disciple and successor, argued that "one should not spell out everything in precise detail, but leave something for the hearer to work out and understand for himself." The Greek critic Demetrius also remarked on the merit of *obscurity* in his study of literary style: "For what is implied is more forceful, and what is explained is thought commonplace."[41]

Such concepts were revived in Europe, though, only in recent centuries. Diderot, the eighteenth century French philosopher and writer, made the following appeal for *obscurity*: "La clarté ne vaut rien pour émouvoir. Poètes, soyez ténébreux." ["Clarity is never enough to move the reader. Poets, be obscure."] The great Italian poet Leopardi repeatedly maintained that poetry should be *vague* and *indefinite*, leaving infinite meanings behind for the reader's imagination to dwell on. The German thinker Schopenhauer also said: "Immer noch besser, etwas Gutes wegzulasssen, als etwas Nichtssagendes hinzulassen. Hier findet das Hesiodische *pléon èmisu pantos*. Überhaupt nicht Alles sagen: *le secret pour être ennuyeux c'est de tout dire*." ["It is better to leave some nice things unspoken than to speak out something insignificant. That is what is meant in the line of Hesiod: *part has more than all*. Never say everything: *the secret of boredom lies in telling everything*."][42]

Among English writers, long before Ezra Pound and the American Imagists, Thomas Carlyle already talked about the wonder of symbol as "silence and speech acting together."[43] Walter Pater also argued that one should always "leave something to the willing intelligence of the reader."[44] Such concepts found their fullest exploration and expression in the symbolist poetics of Poe and Mallarmé, spiritual forefathers of modern Western poetry.

However, the idea of suggestiveness was not necessarily related to the use of images until the age of American Imagism. Although this is a subject beyond the scope of this study, the works of Ezra Pound and Amy Lowell, in particular, and the poetics they advocated at the beginning of their movement, did demonstrate some inspiration from Oriental poetry. But, even in their most representative Imagist poems, images are used less consciously as poetic endings than as a whole, as an entirety. In short, the Imagists did not cultivate a conscious poetics of poetic closure, as Chinese poets did since the High T'ang.[45]

What Aristotle said about tragedy, which he considered "the representation of an action that is complete and whole," has remained true through the centuries for a literary text in general, and has stretched its deep roots into Western poetics:

> Now a whole is that which has a beginning, a middle, and an end. A beginning is that which does not necessarily come after something else, although something else exists or comes about after it. An end, on the contrary, is that which naturally follows something else either as a necessary or as a usual consequence, and is not itself followed by anything.[46]

In short, the sense of *completion, consummation*, and *finality* has become the essence of Western poetic endings, or more appropriately in the Western context, poetic *closure*. As have been pointed out by some critics, it is at the end of a poem "that all the interrelated aspects of theme, the suggestions of imagery, the emotional intensity, the latent demands of logic and the various tonal shadings are brought to some kind of fulfillment and resolved."[47] Poetic endings in Western poetics, then, are points beyond which any further word would be superfluous. They are points of *convergence, conclusion*, and *consummation*.

On the other hand Chinese poetic endings, especially since the innovation in the T'ang brought about the use of scenic closure, frequently aim to create a world beyond the text, or even beyond words, to help enlarge the phenomenological dimensions of a literary text, and make its reading a joined game for both the author and the reader. This may be illustrated by a Ch'an riddle (*gatha*) propounded by the great Sung poet Su Shih:

> If you say it is the lute that makes the music,

Then when encased, why doesn't it make any sound?
If you say the music comes from the fingers,
Then why not listen to your fingers only?[48]

A visual image at the end of a text leaves a lingering vision in the reader's mind after the text comes to an end, inviting the reader to interpret its meaning and its relation with the entire text. It remains a riddle until the reader sets it alive and makes sense out of it, just as the lute has to wait for the musician's fingers to make a beautiful sound. In this sense, then, Chinese poetic closure has often become a point of *departure*, a point for *further exploration*. While there is usually a *centripetal* movement toward the end of a Western poem, the Chinese poem often contains a *centrifugal* movement. One concludes and closes; the other tends to let loose, to provide a new opening, and to release more that lies in potential within a text.

Notes

1. Smith, *Poetic Closure*, vii. Pagination of further references from the book will be given parenthetically in the text.

2. See Joachim Du Bellay, *Oeuvres complètes de Joachim Du Bellay*, ed. par Léon Séché (Paris: Revue de la Renaissance, 4 Vols., 1903–13), III, p. 38. I have also consulted the texts in *Les Antiquitez de Rome* et *Les Regrets*, ed. par E. Droz (Genève: Librairie Droz, 1947), p. 47 and *Les Antiquités de Rome / Les Regrets*, chronologie et introduction par F. Joukovsky (Paris: Garnier-Flammarion, 1971), *Les Regrets*, p. 68. The English translations of all European poems in this chapter are my own.

3. In sharp contrast to the melancholy mood of this text, a poem in the sonnet sequence *Souspirs* by Olivier de Magny, cited in the Droz edition (p. 47, note 4), recounts the joyful experience the three of them were sharing in Italy.

4. Charles-Augustin de Sainte-Beuve, *Notice de l'édition des <Oeuvres> de Joachim du Bellay* chez Victor Pavie, Angers, 1841. Included in Yvonne Bellinger, *Du Bellay: Ses "Regrets" qu'il fit dans Rome: Etude et documentation* (Paris: Nizet, 1975), pp. 333–35.

5. Plato, *Phaedo*, trans. by Benjamin Jowett, from Charles W. Eliot ed. *Plato, Epictetus, Marcus Aurelius* [*The Harvard Classics*] (Danbury, Connecticut: Grolier, 1907, 1980), pp. 45–113. For this citation see p. 77.

6. See T. H. White trans. and ed. *The Bestiary: A Book of Beasts* (New York: Capricorn, 1960), pp. 118–19. Gertrude Jorbes, *Dictionary of Mythology, Folklore and Symbols* (New York: Scarecrow, 2 Vols., 1962), II, pp. 1516–17.

7. M. H. Charmard, in his 1909 critical edition of Du Bellay's works, suggested that this closing image was transposed from a line in Virgil's *Aeneid* (XI, 458), which runs as follows: "dant sonitum rauci per stagna loquacia cycni" ("in hoarse voice the loquacious swans sing over the pond"). See the Droz edition, 158. It is justifiable to some extent, as Du Bellay was indeed conversant with the *Aeneid*, having translated the fourth and sixth books of the epic into French. See Du Bellay, *Oeuvres complètes*, IV, pp. 83–110, 130–62.

8. The cited texts are based upon those from *Catullus: The Poems*, edited with introduction, Revised Text and Commentary by Kenneth Quinn (London: St. Martin's Press, Second Edition, 1973), p. 8, p. 15.

9. This is from *Nachtgesänge* (1803). See Johann Christian Friedrich Hölderlin, *Sämtliche Werke* [Grosse Stuttgarter Ausgabe], Vols. I–V, ed. Friedrich Beissner; Vols. VI–VII, ed. Adolf Beck (Stuttgart: Kohlhammer, Cotta, 1943–77). This poem is in II, Part 1, p. 117. In my English translation of the poem that follows, I have not followed most English translations in which the word *Fahnen* was rendered as *weathervanes*. (There are two translations using respectively *icy flags* and *pennons*.) I deem it better to leave the word in its ambiguity. After all, the Old English origin of the word *vane* is *fana*, very close to the German word in the poem, which means simply *flag*.

10. Martin Heidegger, "Hölderlin and the Essence of Poetry," from Vernon W. Gras ed., *European Literary Theory and Practice: From Existential Phenomenology to Structuralism* (New York: Dell, 1973), pp. 27–41. For the citation see pp. 27–28.

11. Michael Hamburger has argued that *Hälfte des Lebens* articulates the poetics of Imagism by a century earlier. See his essay "1912" in *Contraries: Studies in German Literature* (New York: Dutton, 1970), pp. 263–90. For the observation about the change of poetical orientation see Margaret Gilman, *The Idea of Poetry in France: From Houdar de la Motte to Baudelaire* (Cambridge, Massachusetts: Harvard University Press, 1958), p. 201. For the relation between Stefan George and Hölderlin see an essay by Hans-Georg Gadamer, "Hölderlin und George," in his *Poetica: Ausgewählte Essays* (Frankfurt: Insel Verlag, 1977), pp. 39–68. Stefan George was also an admirer of Mallarmé. See Wallace Fowlie, *Mallarmé* (Chicago: University of Chicago Press, 1953), p. 278.

12. Douglas Bush, *English Poetry: The Main Currents from Chaucer to the Present* (New York: Oxford University Press, 1952, Galaxy Book, 1963), p. 139.

13. See Percy Bysshe Shelley, *Poetical Works*, ed. Thomas Hutchinson (London: Oxford University Press, 1905), p. 550. The poem was first published in *The Examiner* in January 1818, and later reprinted in *Rosalind and Helen* in 1819. The next Shelley poem, *England in 1819* is also cited from this edition (pp. 574–75).

14. Harold Bloom, *The Visionary Company: A Reading of English Romantic Poetry* (New York: Anchor Books, 1963), p. 297.

15. See *The Complete Poetical Works of Percy Bysshe Shelley*, ed. Neville Rogers (London: Oxford University Press, 4 Vols., 1975), *II: 1814–1817*, p. 412.

16. D. W. Harding, "Shelley's Poetry," in Boris Ford ed. *The Pelican Guide to English Literature, V, From Blake to Byron* (Harmondsworth, Middlesex: Penguin, 1962), pp. 207–19. See p. 210.

17. The poem by Guiterman (1871–1945), from his collection *Gaily the Troubadour* (New York: Dutton, 1936), is cited for comparison with *Ozymandias* in X. J. Kennedy's poetry textbook, *An Introduction to Poetry* (Boston: Little, Brown, Third Edition, 1974),

pp. 256–57.

18. See I.A. Richards, *Principles of Literary Criticism* (New York: Harcourt Brace Jovanovich, 1925), esp. XXV, "Badness in Poetry," pp. 199–206.

19. Shelley's *Ozymandias* has been included in such anthologies representing the different tastes of two epochs as Francis Turner Palgrave's *The Golden Treasury* (1861) and *The Norton Anthology of Poetry* (Third Edition, 1983). Desmond King-hele has found that, according to *Granger's Index to Poetry*, which gives a list of anthologies in which any particular poem may be found, *Ozymandias* ranks only after *Ode to the West Wind* and *To a Skylark* as the third most frequently anthologized Shelley poem. See his *Shelley: His Thoughts and Work* (London: Macmillan, 1960), p. 241. I have also found, from my skimming of a considerable number of anthologies, and from consulting the somewhat limited *Hoffman's Index to Poetry*, that Du Bellay's sonnet is one of the more often included in selections of his poetry, and that Hölderlin's *Hälfte des Lebens* definitely belongs to a small group of the author's most frequently anthologized poems. See Herbert H. Hoffman ed., *Hoffman's Index to Poetry: European and Latin American Poetry in Anthologies* (Metuchen, New Jersey: Scarecrow, 1985), p. 112, p. 173.

20. See Raymond Dawson, *The Chinese Chameleon: An Analysis of European Conceptions of Chinese Civilization* (London: Oxford University Press, 1967). Voltaire wrote a play, *L'Orphelin de la Chine*, based on a Jesuit missionary's translation of a Chinese play by the thirteenth century Yüan playwright Chi Chün-hsiang, *The Orphan of the Chao's* (*Chao-shih ku-erh*). Goethe expressed his admiration for several Chinese novels translated by Jesuit missionaries. See the excellent study of the influence of Chinese literature on German writers, Chen Ch'üan's *Chung Te wen-hsüeh yen-chiu* (Shanghai: Shang-wu yin-shu-kuan, 1936). Also see Adolf Reichwein, *China und Europa: Geistige und Künstlerische Beziehungen im 18. Jahrhundert* (Berlin: Oesterheld, 1923).

21. David Hawkes, "Chinese Poetry and the English Reader," in Raymond Dawson ed. *The Legacy of China* (London: Oxford University Press, 1964), pp. 90–115. See also Ch'ien Chung-shu, *T'an yi lu* (Hong Kong: Chung-hua shu-chü, Revised Edition, 1986), pp. 372–73.

22. Paul Verlaine, *Oeuvres posthumes*, II, p. 302 (reprinted from Verlaine's review in *L'Etendue*, 1867). Cited in William Leonard Schwartz, *The Imaginative Interpretation of the Far East in Modern French Literature 1800–1925* (Paris: Librairie ancienne honoré champion, 1927), p. 47. The English translation is mine. Schwartz's book is a thorough study of the limited influence of Chinese literature on French literati of the period. For a study of the influence of Chinese poetry on German literature see Ingrid Schuster, *China und Japan in der deutschen Literatur: 1890–1925* (1977). See also Mary Gertrude Mason, *Western Concepts of China and the Chinese, 1840–1876* (New York, 1939), esp. Chapter IX, "Language and Literature," pp. 174–93.

23. Roy Earl Teele, *Through a Glass Darkly: A Study of English Translations of Chinese Poetry*, Ph.D. dissertation, Columbia University (Ann Arbor, Michigan, 1949).

24. Victor de Laprade, "Les Poètes classiques de la Chine," *Le Correspondant* (Paris, 1864), pp. 413–34. Cited in Mason, p. 192.

25. W. H. Medhurst, "Chinese Poetry: A Lecture Delivered at Shanghai," in *The China Review*, Vol. IV (July and August 1875), pp. 46–56.

26. V. W. W. S. Purcell, *The Spirit of Chinese Poetry: An Original Essay* (Singapore:

Kelly and Walsh, 1929), p. 18.

27. Teele, p. 95.

28. There are, strictly speaking, a few exceptions to this. One of the few was Friedrich Rückert (1788–1866), a German professor of Oriental languages who was also a poet himself. He was known for his translations from Arabic and Sanskrit as well as his own lyric poems, many of which were set into music by Brahms, Schubert and Mahler. Rückert did not know Chinese, but in 1833 he translated into German (from a Latin translation entitled *La Charme*, 1733) the *Shih-ching*, which remained in manuscript form until 1830, when it was published by Julius Mohl. See Mason, p. 189. The other exception was Judith (Gautier) Walter (1845–1917), whose translation *Livre de jade* was praised by Arthur Waley for its "beauty." See Waley trans. *A Hundred and Seventy Chinese Poems* (London: Constable, 1918), *Bibliographical Notes*, pp. 21–22.

29. For a biographical note about Herbert A. Giles (1845–1935) see the "Introduction to the New Edition" by Terence Barrow to Giles, *A History of Chinese Literature* (Rutland, Vermont: Charles E. Tuttle, 1901, New Edition, 1973). See also Fei Sheng-ling, "One Generation of Chinese Studies in Cambridge: An Appreciation of Professor H. A. Giles," *Chinese Social and Political Science Review*, XV (1931), pp. 79–89. For Waley's remark, see *Bibliographical Notes* in his *A Hundred and Seventy Chinese Poems*, pp. 21–22.

30. Here Giles is still talking about the "stop-shorts" or the Chinese quatrain (*chüeh-chü*) in regulated verse.

31. Giles, *History*, pp. 145–46.

32. One of such examples, Po Chü-yi's *A Visit to the Wu-chen Temple: 130 Rhymed Couplets* (*Yu Wu-chen shih yi-pai san-shih yün*), which runs to 260 lines in length, appeared in Arthur Waley's translation, entitled simply as *The Temple*, in 1923. See Waley, *The Temple and Other Poems* (New York: Knopf, 1923), pp. 103–12. W. B. Yeats liked the poem so much that he included it in the anthology that he compiled, *The Oxford Book of Modern Verse, 1892–1935* (London: Oxford University Press, 1936), pp. 247–56.

33. Strachey read Giles's anthology in June 1907 and observed that Chinese poetry was "one of the most charming in the world." The next year he took the book with him during a trip to Scotland and started working on the review, which he published in *The New Quarterly* in October that year. See Michael Holroyd, *Lytton Strachey: A Critical Biography* (London: Heinemann, 2 Vols., 1967), I, p. 317, pp. 345–47. For Strachey's opinion of Yeats see his essay "Modern Poetry," *The Spectator*, 100 (April 18, 1908), pp. 622–23.

34. Strachey, "An Anthology," *New Quarterly* I (October 1908), pp. 603–610. The essay was reprinted in *Characters and Commentaries* (New York: Harcourt Brace, 1933), pp. 138–146. Although Strachey did not mention it, he must have also read Giles's *A History of Chinese Literature*. Unlike Giles, though, Strachey did not restrict the Chinese critic's remarks ("The words stop, but the sense goes on") within the field of the "stop-shorts" only. It should also be noted here that, since most of the surviving Greek lyrics are fragments, frequently containing flashes of images, their effect on the reader is anything but of completeness. Thus Greek lyrics are far closer to Chinese poetics than most later Western poetry. The italicization of some words in the quotation is mine.

35. Waley, "Our Debt to China," *Asiatic Review*, XXXVI (July 1940), p. 554. Such

a preference for shorter forms as Waley described actually represents, it seems to me, one line of Western poetics that started in recent centuries, such as that found in the words of Leopardi, Baudelaire, Joseph Joubert, and Edgar Allan Poe. See Ch'ien Chung-shu, *T'an yi lu*, pp. 619–20.

36. Virginia Woolf, "Mr. Bennett and Mrs. Brown," reprinted in Robert Scholes ed., *Approaches to the Novel: Materials for a Poetics* (San Francisco: Chandler, 1961), pp. 211–30; for this citation see pp. 212–13. In a similar way, Michael Hamburger also asserted that the year 1912 was a kind of *annus mirabilis* in the history of modern German poetry. See his *Contraries*, pp. 263–90.

37. Wai-lim Yip has provided a list of mainly English translations of Chinese poetry in chronological order in his *Ezra Pound's Cathay* (Princeton: Princeton University Press, 1969), pp. 244–49. To cite just one example of the popularity of Chinese poetry here: Arthur Waley's *A Hundred and Seventy Chinese Poems* went through twelve reprints in England, and nine in America, within the next three decades after its first publication in 1918. See Francis A. Johns, *A Bibliography of Arthur Waley* (New Brunswick, New Jersey: Rutgers University Press, 1968), pp. 17–18.

38. Waley, "Introduction to *A Hundred and Seventy Chinese Poems* (1962 Edition)," dated 1960, included in Ivan Morris ed., *Madly Singing in the Mountains: An Appreciation and Anthology of Arthur Waley* (New York: Walker, 1970), pp. 131–37; for this quote see pp. 135–36.

39. Purcell, p. 2.

40. Heidegger, p. 27.

41. The remarks of Theophrastus were cited by Demetrius in the latter's work, *On Style* (222). Demetrius's own remark is also from the work (254). See G. M. A. Grube, *A Greek Critic: Demetrius on Style* (Toronto: University of Toronto Press, 1961), p. 111, p. 117.

42. Denis Diderot, "Salon de 1767," *Oeuvres complètes*, ed. Assézat et Tourneux, XI, p. 147. Giacomo Leopardi, *Zibaldone*, Mondadori, I, 86, 105, 126, 382, 971, 1145; II, 1128. Arthur Schopenhauer, *Parerga und Parelipomena*, Kap. 13, 283, from *Sämtliche Werke*, ed. P. Deussen, V, 570. The line of Hesiod cited by Schopenhauer is line 40 from *Works and Days*. The French citation is in No. 6 of Voltaire's poem *Sur l'Homme*. These were quoted by Ch'ien Chung-shu in his discussion on the Chinese term *shen-yün* ("spirit and tone") in *Kuan chui p'ien*, IV, pp. 1359–1361. All the English translations here are mine.

43. Thomas Carlyle, *Sartor Resartus*, III, ch. 3. This is quoted by Ch'ien Chung-shu in his *T'an yi lu*, p. 309.

44. Walter Pater, "Style," in Harold Bloom ed. *Selected Writings of Walter Pater* (New York: Signet, 1974), pp. 103–24; for this quotation see p. 110.

45. On several occasions the Imagists came very close to the Chinese poetics of the scenic closure. Ezra Pound's rearrangement of a Giles translation, "Liu Ch'e," captures the essence of the image ending since the T'ang, though the original, mistakenly attributed to the Emperor Wu-ti of the Han, was an earlier text. For an interesting comparison of the two texts of Giles and Pound see Yip, 64. For the influence of East Asian poetry on Pound see especially Yip's book, and also Earl Miner, "Pound, *Haiku*, and the Image," in Walter Sutton ed., *Ezra Pound: A Collection of Critical Essays* (Englewood Cliffs, New Jersey: Prentice-Hall, 1963), pp. 115–28.

46. Aristotle, *Poetics*, ch. 7, in T. S. Dorsch trans. *Classical Literary Criticism: Aristotle, Horace, Longinus* (Harmondsworth, Middlesex: Penguin, 1965), pp. 29–76; for this quotation see p. 41.

47. Peter Broome and Graham Chesters, *The Appreciation of Modern French Poetry: 1850–1950* (Cambridge: Cambridge University Press, 1976), p. 47.

48. This is from Su Shih's "A Letter to Administrative Assistant Yen-cheng" (*Yü Yen-cheng p'an-kuan shu*). See *Su Shih wen-chi*, ed. by K'ung Fan-li (Peking: Chung-hua shu-chü, 6 Vols., 1986), IV, (*chüan* 57), p. 1729.

Glossary

An Lu-shan (d. 757) 安祿山

Chan kuo ts'e 戰國策
Ch'an (Zen) 禪
Chang Chiu-ling (678–740) 張九齡
Chang chü 章句
Chang Shao-kang 張少康
ch'ang 暢
Ch'ang-an 長安
Ch'ang ko hsing 長歌行
Chao-jung 昭容
Chao Yen-ts'ai (Sung) 趙彥材
Chen-kuan (627–49) 貞觀
Ch'en Chi (8th c.) 陳季
Ch'en Shih-tao (1053–1102) 陳師道
Ch'en Tzu-ang (661–702) 陳子昂
cheng 正
Cheng-chien 鄭箋
Cheng Chung (d. 83) 鄭重
Cheng Hsüan (127–200) 鄭玄
chi 雞
Chi Chün-hsiang (13th–14th c.) 紀君祥
chi shih hsing le 及時行樂
chi t'o shen yüan 寄託深遠
Chi Yu-kung (12th c.) 計有功
ch'i 起
ch'i 氣
Ch'i 齊
Ch'i Chi (863?–937?) 齊己
ch'i chieh 起結
Ch'i-yü 淇奧
Chia-jen 佳人
Chia Tao (779-843) 賈島
Chia Yi (201-169 B.C.) 賈誼
Chiang K'uei (1155?–1221?) 姜夔
Ch'iang 羌
Chiao-liao 椒聊
chiao-jung 交融
chieh 節
chieh chü 結句
ch'ieh chih 切至
Chien-an (196–219) 建安
Chien-chia 蒹葭
Chien-k'ang 建康
chien chü 健舉
Chien-wen-ti (Liang) 梁簡文帝 (See Hsiao Kang)
Ch'ien Ch'i (722–80) 錢起
Ch'ien Chung-shu 錢鍾書
chih 志
chih ch'en ch'i shih 直陳其事
chih-chü 旨趣
chih-yin 知音
Chih Yü (d. 311) 摯虞

Chin 晉
Chin Sheng-t'an (1608–61) 金聖嘆
chin-shih 進士
Chin shu 晉書
Ch'in 秦
ch'in 侵
ching 景
ching-ch'e 警策
ching chieh 境界
ching ju li 景入理
ching-lien 頸聯
Ching-nü 靜女
ching wu 景物
Ch'ing 清
ch'ing 青
ch'ing 情
ch'ing ching chiao-jung 情景交融
Ch'iu-feng tz'u 秋風辭
Chiu-ji Lan-t'ien Ts'ui-shih chuang 九日藍田崔氏莊
chiu shuo 舊說
Chiu T'ang shu 舊唐書
Chiu-yi shan 九嶷山
Chou 周
Chou-li 周禮
ch'ou 愁
Chu 著
Chu Hsi (1130–1200) 朱熹
Chu Tzu-ch'ing (1898-1948) 朱自清
chu-yü 茱萸
Ch'u 楚
Ch'u sai 出塞
ch'u shih 出世
Ch'u-tz'u 楚辭
chü chiu 雎鳩
chü-fa 句法
Ch'ü Yüan (340?–278? B.C.) 屈原
chüan 卷
Chuangtzu 莊子
chüeh chü 絕句
chün pu chien 君不見
chün-tzu 君子
ch'üan-tien 圈點
Chung Hung (468?–518) 鍾嶸
Chung-tsung (T'ang) (Ruled 683, 705–10) 唐中宗
Chung-yung 中庸
Confucius (K'ung Ch'iu) (551–479 B.C.) 孔夫子(孔丘)

e-tu 阿堵
Erh-Nan mi-chih 二南祕旨
Erh-shih-ssu shih-p'in 二十四詩品

Fan Hsi-wen (13th c.) 范晞文
fang k'ai 放開
Fei hu hsing 飛鶻行
Fen 汾(水)
Feng 風
fu 附
fu 縛
fu 賦

Fu chi hsing 縛雞行
Fu-chou 鄜州
Fu-hui 附會

Hai-jo 海若
han 含
Han 漢
han-hsü 含蓄
han-lien 頷聯
Han-shu 漢書
Han-shui 漢水
han ssu lo chü shih 含思落句
Han Yü (768–824) 韓愈
Heng-t'ang lu 橫塘路
ho 何
Ho Chu (1052–1125) 賀鑄
ho sheng 和聲
Ho ts'ao pu huang 何草不黃
Hsi K'ang (210–63) 嵇康
Hsi ko 西閣
Hsi-tz'u 繫辭
Hsi wei liu chüeh-chü 戲為六絕句
hsia 下
Hsiang 湘(江)
Hsiang ling ku se 湘靈鼓瑟
hsiao erh nü 小兒女
Hsiao-hsü 小序
Hsiao Kang 蕭綱
(Emperor Chien-wen-ti of Liang, 503–51, ruled 549–55)
Hsiao-min 小閔
Hsiao-ya 小雅
Hsieh An (320–85) 謝安
Hsieh Chen (1495–1575) 謝榛
hsieh-ching 寫景
Hsieh Hsüan (343–88) 謝玄
Hsin Ch'i-chi (1140–1207) 辛棄疾
hsing 行
hsing 興
hsing ch'ü 興趣
Hsü Fu-kuan 徐復觀
Hsü Kan (171–218) 徐幹
Hsü Yin (9th–10th c.) 徐寅
Hsüan Tsung (T'ang) 唐玄宗
(685–762, ruled 712–56)
hsüan-yen shih 玄言詩
Hu 胡
Hu Shih (1891–1962) 胡適
hu ts'ang ch'i chai 互藏其宅
Hu Ying-ling (1551–1602) 胡應麟
hua she t'ien chu 畫蛇添足
Huainantzu 淮南子
huai ts'ai pu yü 懷才不遇
huan 歡
Huang Ch'e (12th c.) 黃徹
Huang-ti 黃帝
Huang T'ing-chien (1045–1105) 黃庭堅
Huang-yi 皇矣
Hui-neng (638–713) 惠能
Hunan 湖南
hun-mang 混茫
Hung-chou 洪州

Hung Mai (1123–1202) 洪邁

I-ching (*Book of Changes*) 易經

jen 仁
Jen chien hsün 人間訓
ju 如
ju-ching 儒經
ju shen 入神
ju shih 入世
Juan Chi (210–63) 阮籍

k'ai meng chien shan 開門見山
K'ai-yüan (713-41) 開元
Kao Shih (706?–65) 高適
Kiangsi 江西
Ko Li-fang (d. 1164) 葛立方
Kōbō Daishi (774–835) 弘法大師
(Monk KūKai) (空海)
Kōzen Hiroshi 興膳宏
k'ou mi fu chien 口蜜腹劍
ku 骨
Ku K'ai-chih (345?–406) 顧愷之
ku shih 古詩
Ku-shih shih-chiu-shou 古詩十九首
ku-tzu 骨子
Ku Yen-wu (1613–82) 顧炎武
Kuan-chü 關雎
Kuei-ch'ü-lai tz'u 歸去來辭
K'uei-chou 夔州
Kung Liu 公劉
kung-ming 功名
Kung-sun Ni-tzu (5th c. B.C.)
公孫尼子
K'ung Ying-ta (574–648) 孔穎達
Kwangsi 廣西

Lan-shui 藍水
le chi sheng pei 樂極生悲
li 理
li 里
Li-chi 禮記
Li Ch'iao (644–713) 李嶠
li ju ching 理入情
Li Ling (d. 74 B. C.) 李陵
Li Lin-fu (d. 752) 李林甫
Li Po (701–62) 李白
Li-sao 離騷
Li Te-yüan (N. Sung) 李德遠
Li Tung-yang (1447–1516) 李東陽
Li Yen-nien (d. 87? B.C.) 李延年
Liang 梁
Liang ching fu 兩京賦
Liehtzu 列子
Liu Ch'en-weng (1232–97) 劉辰翁
Liu Hsi-tsai (1813–81) 劉熙載
Liu Hsi-yi (651–80?) 劉希夷
Liu Hsieh (465?–520?) 劉勰
liu shih 六詩
Liu Tsung-yüan (773–819) 柳宗元

liu tuan 六斷
liu yi 六義
lo chü 落句
Lo-yu Yüan ko 樂遊原歌
Lu Chao-ling (635?–89?) 盧照鄰
Lu Chi (261–303) 陸機
Lu Chung-lien 魯仲連 (4th–3rd c. B.C.)
lü-shih 律詩
Lü-shih ch'un-ch'iu 呂氏春秋
Lü-yeh shu-huai 旅夜書懷

Mao Ch'ang (W. Han) 毛萇
Mao Heng (W. Han) 毛亨
Mao Shih 毛詩
Mei Yao-ch'en (1002–60) 梅堯臣
Meng Chia (4th c.) 孟嘉
Meng Hao-jan (689–740) 孟浩然
Mien 綿
Ming 明
ming 名
ming hsing 明星
Ming shih 明詩
mu 目

nei 內

Ou-yang Hsiu (1007–72) 歐陽修

Pa ai shih 八哀詩
pa-ping 八病
Pai-shih Tao-jen shih-shuo 白石道人詩說
Pan Ku (32–92) 班固
P'an Yüeh (247–300) 潘岳
pei 悲
Pei ko 悲歌
pi 比
pi fang yü wu 比方於物
p'i-p'a 琵琶
Piao yu mei 摽有梅
p'ien chung 篇終
P'ing-yi 馮夷
Po-chou 柏舟
Po Chü-yi (772–846) 白居易
Po-liang t'ai 柏梁臺
p'o-t'i 破題
pu 不
pu chin yi 不盡意

sai weng shih ma 塞翁失馬
san-ching 三經
San-fu huang-t'u 三輔黃圖
san-wei 三緯
Shan-hai-ching 山海經
Shan-hsing 善行
Shang-kuan Wan-erh (664–710) 上官婉兒
Shang-kuan Yi (616?–64) 上官儀
Shang-shu 尚書

shen 神

Shen Ch'üan-ch'i (656?–714) 沈佺期

Shen Yi-fu (12th–13th c.) 沈義父

Shen Yüeh (385–433) 沈約

shen yün 神韻

sheng 生

Sheng-min 生民

sheng T'ang 盛唐

sheng T'ang chih yin 盛唐之音

shih 詩

shih 事

shih 勢

Shih-chi 史記

Shih-ch'i shih 十七勢

Shih-ching 詩經

Shih-chung mi-chih 詩中祕旨

shih hua 詩話

Shih-ko 詩格

Shih k'o yi hsing 詩可以興

Shih-p'in 詩品

Shih-shuo hsin-yü 世說新語

Shih-sou 詩藪

shih-t'ieh shih 試帖詩

shih-wei 詩尾

shih-yen 詩眼

shou-lien 首聯

shuang 雙

ssu-sheng 四聲

Sung 宋

Sung 頌

Szechuan 四川

Ssu-k'ung T'u (837–908) 司空圖

Ssu-ma Hsiang-ju (179–117 B.C.) 司馬相如

Ssu-ma Jang-chü (6th–5th c. B.C.) 司馬穰苴

Su Shih (1037–1101) 蘇軾

Su Wu (d. 60 B.C.) 蘇武

Sung Chih-wen (656?–712) 宋之問

Ta-hsü (*Great Preface*) *大序*

"Ta Hung Chü-fu shu" 答洪駒父書

Ta-li (766–79) 大歷

Ta-ming 大明

ta-shih 大師

Ta-ya 大雅

T'ang 唐

T'ang-jen shih-lü shuo 唐人試律說

T'ang-shih chi-shih 唐詩紀事

T'ang-wen 湯問

Tao 道

T'ao Ch'ien (365?–427) 陶潛

T'ao-yao 桃夭

te shih 得失

Ti-tung 蝃蝀

t'i 體

t'i-mu 題目

tiao-tu 調度

tien t'ieh ch'eng chin 點鐵成金

t'ien chi 天機

T'ien tao 天道

t'o shih yü wu 託事於物

t'o wu ch'i hsing 託物起興
t'o yü 託喻
Ts'ai-fan 採蘩
Ts'ai ko 採葛
Ts'ai sang tzu 採桑子
Ts'ai wei 採薇
ts'an-chün 參軍
Ts'ang-lang 滄浪
Ts'ang-wu 蒼梧
Ts'ao Chih (192–232) 曹植
Ts'ao P'i 曹丕
(Emperor Wen-ti of Wei, 187–226, ruled 220–26)
Ts'ao Ts'ao (155–220) 曹操
Ts'en Shen (714?–20) 岑參
Tso Ssu (250?–305?) 左思
tu 獨
Tu Fu (712–70) 杜甫
Tu li 獨立
T'u-chü 兔苴
tuan chang ch'ü yi 斷章取義
tuan chü 斷句
Tung hsi ch'uan hsing 東西船行
Tung-meng chih yang 東門之楊
T'ung-ch'üeh t'ai 銅雀臺
tzu-yen 字眼
tz'u 詞
tz'u 辭

wai 外
wai-wu 外物
wang 望
Wang Ch'ang-ling (698?–756?) 王昌齡
Wang-ch'uan 輞川
Wang Fu-chih (1619–92) 王夫之
Wang Kuo-wei (1877–1927)王國維
Wang Po (650–77) 王勃
Wang Shih-chen (1526–90) 王世貞
Wang Shih-chen (1634–1711) 王士禎
Wang Wei (701–61) 王維
Wang Yi (2nd c.) 王逸
Wei 魏
wei chü 尾句
wei-lien 尾聯
Wei Ts'ui (8th c.) 魏璀
wen 文
Wen-chang liu-pieh-lun 文章流別論
Wen-ching mi-fu-lun 文鏡祕府論
Wen-fu 文賦
Wen-hsin tiao-lung 文心雕龍
Wen-hsüan 文選
Wen T'ing-yün (812?–66) 溫庭筠
wen-wai chih ch'ung-chih 文外之重旨
wen yi chin erh yi yu yü 文已盡而意有餘
Wen Yü (10th c.) 文彧
wo 我
wu 物
wu hsin 無心
Wu se 物色

Wu-ti (Han) (156–87B.C., ruled 141–87 B.C.) 漢武帝
Wu-ti pen-chi 武帝本紀
Wu Yin 戊寅

Yangtze 揚子(江); 長江
Yao-tien 堯典
Yeh yu man-ts'ao 野有蔓草
Yeh yu ssu-chün 野有死麇
yen 眼
Yen Wei (8th c.) 嚴維
Yen Wu (726–65) 嚴武
Yen Yü (ca. 13th c.) 嚴羽
yi 意
yi Ch'ang-an 憶長安
yi ching chieh ch'ing 以景結情
yi-lun 議論
Yi-wen-chih 藝文志
yin 隱
yu kan chih tz'u 有感之詞
Yu Wu-chen shih yi-pai san-shih yün 游悟真寺一百三十韻
"Yü Yen-cheng p'an-kuan shu" 與彥正判官書
yu yüan shen 有遠神
Yü-fu 漁父
Yü-shan 玉山
Yü Shih-nan (558–638) 虞世南
Yü-weng 漁翁
yüan 怨
Yüan 元
Yüan-yu 遠遊
Yüeh-chi 樂記
yüeh-fu 樂府
Yüeh-fu chih-mi 樂府指迷
Yüeh yeh 月夜
Yün-t'ai shan 雲臺山
Yung-huai 詠懷
yung-kung 用功
Yung-shih shih 詠史詩
yung-wu shih 詠物詩

Bibliography

Works in Chinese

Chao Chih-yang. *Shih-ching fu pi hsing chung-lun*. Hsin-chu: Feng-ch'eng shu-chü, 1974.

Ch'en Hang. *Shih pi hsing chien*. Preface by Wei Yüan 1854. Shanghai: Chung-hua shu-chü, 1959.

Ch'en Ch'üan. *Chung Te wen-hsüeh yen-chiu*. Shanghai: Shang-wu yin-shu-kuan, 1936.

Cheng Yü-ch'ing. *Shih chi ch'uan chih fu pi hsing yen-chiu*. Taipei: Wen-ching ch'u-pan-she, 1976.

Ch'eng-yü tz'u-tien. Ed. by the Bureau of Education of Ch'ang-chou. Nan-king: Chiang-su jen-min ch'u-pan-she, 1981.

Chi Yu-kung. *T'ang-shih chi-shih*. 1224, 81 *chüan*. Shanghai: Chung-hua shu-chü, 1965. 2 Vols.

——. *T'ang-shih chi-shih chiao-chien*. Ed. by Wang Chung-yung, Ch'eng-tu: Pa-Shu shu-she, 1989. 2 Vols.

Chi Yün. *T'ang-jen shih-lü shuo*. 1699. Revised Edition 1700. *Kuo-ch'ao ming-jen chu-shu ts'ung-shu, IX*. Shanghai: Sung-yin ko, 1879. 10 Vols.

Chiang Shan-kuo. *San-pai-p'ien yen-lun*. Shanghai: Shang-wu yin-shu-kuan, 1931.

Ch'ien Chung-shu. *Chiu-wen ssu-p'ien*. Shanghai: Ku-chi ch'u-pan-she, 1979.

——. *Kuan chui p'ien*. Peking: Chung-hua shu-chü, 1979. 4 Vols.

——. *Kuan chui p'ien tseng-ting*. Peking: Chung-hua shu-chü, 1982.

——. ed. *Sung-shih hsüan-chu*. Peking: Jen-min wen-hsüeh ch'u-pan-she, 1958. Reprint. Szechuan: Ch'ung-ch'ing ch'u-pan-she, 1982.

——. *T'an yi lu*. Revised Edition. Hong Kong: Chung-hua shu-chü, 1986.

Chin Sheng-t'an. *Tu-shih chieh*. Ed. by Chung Lai-yin. Shanghai: Ku-chi ch'u-pan-she, 1984.

Chin shu. Fang Hsüan-ling et al. Peking: Chung-hua shu-chü, 1974. 12 Vols.

Chiu T'ang shu. Liu Hsü et al. Peking: Chung-hua shu-chü, 1975. 16 Vols.

Chou Chen-fu. *Shih-tz'u li-hua*. Second Edition. Peking: Chung-kuo ch'ing-nien ch'u-pan-she, 1979.

——. *Wen-chang li-hua*. Peking: Chung-kuo ch'ing-nien ch'u-pan-she, 1983.

Chu Hsi. *Chu-tzu yü-lei*. Ed. by Li Ching-te. New Punctuated Edition by Wang Hsing-hsien. Peking: Chung-hua shu-chü, 1986. 8 Vols.

——. *Shih chi ch'uan*. Shanghai: Chung-hua shu-chü, 1958.

——. *Ssu-shu chi-chu*. Shanghai: Shih-chieh shu-chü, 1937.

Chu Tzu-ch'ing. *Chu Tzu-ch'ing ku-tien wen-hsüeh lun-wen-chi*. Shanghai: Ku-chi ch'u-pan-she, 1981. 2 Vols.

Ch'u-tz'u chu-shih. Ed. by Ma Mao-yüan et al. Hsien-ning: Hupei jen-min ch'u-pan-she, 1985.

Ch'üan Tang shih. 1705, 900 *chüan*. Peking: Chung-hua shu-chü, 1985. 25 Vols.

Fang Yü-jun. *Shih-ching yüan shih*. Ed. by Li Hsien-keng. Peking: Chung-hua shu-chü, 1986. 2 Vols.

Hsien-Ch'in Han Wei Chin nan-pei-ch'ao shih. Ed. by Lu Ch'in-li. Peking: Chung-hua shu-chü, 1983. 3 Vols.

Hsien-Ch'in wen-hsüeh-shih ts'an-k'ao tzu-liao. Ed. by the Teaching and Research Group of the History of Chinese Literature, Peking University. Peking: Chung-hua shu-chü, 1962.

Ho Wen-huan ed. *Li-tai shih-hua*. Preface 1770. Peking: Chung-hua shu-chü, 1981. 2 Vols.

Hsin T'ang shu. Ou-yang Hsiu et al. Peking: Chung-hua shu-chü, 1975.

Hsü Fu-kuan. *Chung-kuo wen-hsüeh lun-chi*. Revised Edition. Taipei: Taiwan hsüeh-sheng shu-chü, 1974.

Hu Chen-heng. *T'ang-yin k'uei-ch'ien*. Ed. by Chou Pen-ch'un. Shanghai: Ku-chi ch'u-pan-she, 1981.

Hu Shih. *Pai-hua wen-hsüeh shih*. Fourth Edition. Ch'ang-sha: Shang-wu yin-shu-kuan, 1938.

Hua Wen-hsüan ed. *Ku-tien wen-hsüeh yen-chiu tzu-liao hui-pien: Tu Fu chüan*. Peking: Chung-hua shu-chü, 1964. 3 Vols.

Huang Yung-wu. ed. *Tu Fu shih-chi ssu-shih chung so-yin*. Taipei: Ta-t'ung shu-chü, 1976.

Kōbō Daishi compiled. *Wen-ching mi-fu-lun (Bunkyo hifuron) chiao-chu*. Ed., annotated and with commentary by Wang Li-chi. Peking: Chung-kuo she-hui k'o-hsüeh ch'u-pan-she, 1983.

Ku Chieh-kang ed. *Ku shih pien*. Vol. III. Peking: Peking shu-chü, 1937.

K'ung Ying-ta. *Li-chi chu-shu*. *Ssu-pu pei-yao* Edition, 63 *chüan*. Reprint. Shanghai: Chung-hua shu-chü, 1933. 14 Vols.

Kuo Shao-yü and Wang Wen-sheng eds. *Chung-kuo li-tai wen-lun hsüan*. Shanghai: Ku chi ch'u-pan-she, 1979. 4 Vols.

Kuo Shao-yü. *Sung shih-hua k'ao*. Peking: Chung-hua shu-chü, 1979.

Liang-Han wen-hsüeh shih ts'an-k'ao tzu-liao. Ed. by the Teaching and Research Group of the History of Chinese Literature, Peking University. Peking: Chung-hua shu-chü, 1962.

Ling Tze-lou. *T'ang shih hsüan-pen Tu Fu shih ts'ai hsüan t'ung chi (A Statistical Study of Selected Poems of Tu Fu)*. Hong Kong: Chu Hai College, 1970.

Liu Hsi-tsai. *Yi kai*. Preface 1873. 1927. Reprint. Taipei: Kuang-wen ch'u-pan-she, 1964.

Liu Hsieh. *Wen-hsin tiao-lung chu-shih*. Ed. and annotated by Chou Chen-fu. Peking: Jen-min wen-hsüeh ch'u-pan-she, 1981.

Liu Meng-k'ang. *Tu Fu nien-p'u*. Hong Kong: Hua-hsia ch'u-pan-she, 1967.

Liu Yi-ch'ing. *Shih-shuo hsin-yü chiao-chien*. Ed. by Hsü Cheng-o. Peking: Chung-hua shu-chü, 1984. 2 Vols.

Lu Chi. *Wen-fu chi-shih*. Ed. by Chang Shao-k'ang. Shanghai: Ku-chi ch'u-pan-she, 1984.

Ma Mao-yüan. *Ku-shih shih-chiu-shou t'an-so*. Peking: Tso-chia ch'u-pan-she, 1957.

Mao Shih. *Ssu-pu pei-yao* Edition. Reprint. Shanghai: Chung-hua shu-chü, undated. 4 Vols.

P'ing-chu Chao-ming Wen-hsüan. Ed. by Yü Kuang-hua. 1778. Reprint. Taipei: Hsüeh-hai ch'u-pan-she, 1981.

Shen Te-ch'üan. *Shuo-shih ts'ui-yü ch'üan-p'ing*. Ed. with commentary by Su Wen-cho. Hong Kong: Chih-hao shu-chü, 1978.

Shen Yi-fu. *Yüeh-fu chih-mi*. T'ang Kuei-chang ed. *Tz'u-hua ts'ung-pien*. 1934. 12 Vols. Reprint. Taipei: Kuang-wen ch'u-pan-she, 1967, I: pp. 229–47.

Shih-ching p'ing-chu tu-pen. Ed. by P'ei P'u-hsien. Taipei: San-min shu-chü, 1982. 2 Vols.

T'ang-shih chien-shang tz'u-tien. Ed. by Hsiao T'i-fei et al. Shanghai: Tz'u-shu ch'u-pan-she, 1983.

Ting Fu-pao ed. *Li-tai shih-hua hsüan-pien*. Reprint. Peking: Chung-hua shu-chü, 1983. 3 Vols.

Ting Hsiu-hui. *Liu Ho-tung chi pien-nien hsi-chu*. M. A. Thesis, National Taiwan Normal University, 1974.

Tu Fu. *Chiu-chia chi-chu Tu-shih*. Ed. by Kuo Chih-ta. 1181. *Ssu-k'u ch'üan-shu pen* Edition. 1788. Reprint. Taipei: Ta-t'ung ch'u-pan-she, 1974. 5 Vols.

——. *Tu-shih ching-ch'üan*. Ed. by Yang Lun. (Preface 1791). Shanghai: Ku-chi ch'u-pan-she, 1962. 2 Vols.

Tz'u hai. Shanghai: Tz'u-shu ch'u-pan-she, 1979.

Tz'u yüan. Revised Edition. Hong Kong: Shang-wu yin-shu-kuan, 1981. 4 Vols.

Wang Ta-p'eng et al. eds. *Chung-kuo li-tai shih-hua hsüan*. Ch'ang-sha: Yüeh-lu shu-she, 1985. 2 Vols.

Wang Fu-chih. *Chiang-chai shih-hua chien-chu*. Ed. and annotated by Tai Hung-sen. Peking: Jen-min wen-hsüeh ch'u-pan-she, 1981.

Wang Li. *Han-yü shih-lü hsüeh*. Second Edition. Shanghai: Chiao-yü ch'u-pan-she, 1979.

Wang Wei. *Wang Yu-ch'eng chi chien-chu*. Ed. by Chao Tien-ch'eng. *Ssu-pu pei-yao* Edition, 1737. Reprint. Shanghai: Chung-hua shu-chü, undated. 4 Vols.

Wang Yüan-hua ed. *Jih-pen yen-chiu Wen-hsin tiao-lung lun-wen-chi*. Chi-nan: Ch'i-lu shu-she, 1983.

Wei Chin nan-pei-ch'ao wen-hsüeh-shih ts'an-k'ao tzu-liao. Ed. by the Teaching and Research Group of the History of Chinese Literature, Peking University. Peking; Chung-hua shu-chü, 1962. 2 Vols.

Wei Ch'ing-chih ed. *Shih-jen yü-hsieh*. Preface 1244. Shanghai: Ku-chi ch'u-pan-she, 1978. 2 Vols.

Yao Chi-heng. *Shih-ching t'ung-lun*. Ed. by Ku Chieh-kang. Reprint: Shanghai, Chung-hua shu-chü, 1958.

Works in Western Languages

Barthes, Roland. *Image-Music-Text*. Essays selected and translated by Stephen Heath. New York: Hill and Wang, 1977.

——. *Le Plaisir du texte*. Paris: Seuil, 1973.

Bellinger, Yvonne. *Du Bellay: Ses "Regrets" qu'il fit dans Rome*. Paris: Nizet, 1975.

Birch, Cyril ed. *Studies in Chinese Literary Genres*. Berkeley: University of California Press, 1974.

Bloom, Harold ed. *Percy Bysshe Shelley: Modern Critical Views*. New York: Chelsea House, 1985.

——. *The Visionary Company: A Reading of English Romantic Poetry*. Garden City, New York: Doubleday, 1963.

Broome, Peter and Chesters, Graham. *The Appreciation of Modern French Poetry (1850–1950)*. Cambridge: Cambridge University Press, 1976.

Bush, Douglas. *English Poetry: The Main Currents from Chaucer to the Present*. New York: Oxford University Press, 1952. Galaxy Book, 1963.

Bush, Susan and Christian Murck eds. *Theories of the Arts in China*. Princeton: Princeton University Press, 1983.

Byron, George Gordon. *Poetical Works*. London: Oxford University Press, 1904, 1945.

Catullus. *The Poems*. Ed. with Introduction, Revised Text and Commentary by Kenneth Quinn. Second Edition. London: St. Martin's Press, 1973.

Chang, Kang-i Sun. *Six Dynasties Poetry*. Princeton: Princeton University Press, 1986.

Chang, Kwang-chih. *The Archeology of Ancient China*. New Haven: Yale University Press, 1969.

——. (K. C.). *Art, Myth, and Ritual: The Path to Political Authority in Ancient China*. Cambridge, Massachusetts: Harvard University Press, 1983.

Chen, Shih-hsiang. "The *Shih-ching*: Its Generic Significance in Chinese Literary History and Poetics." Cyril Birch ed. *Studies in Chinese Literary Genres* (Berkeley: University of California Press, 1974): pp. 8–41.

Classical Literary Criticism: Aristotle, Horace, Longinus. Tr. by T. S. Dorsch. Harmondsworth, Middlesex: Penguin Books, 1963.

Culler, Jonathan. *Structuralist Poetics: Structuralism, Linguistics, and the Study of Literature*. Ithaca: Cornell University Press, 1975.

Davis, A.R. *Tu Fu*. Hew York: Twayne, 1971.

Dawson, Raymond. *The Chinese Chameleon: An Analysis of European*

Conceptions of Chinese Civilizations. London: Oxford University Press, 1967.

—— ed. *The Legacy of China*. London: Oxford University Press, 1964.

Deeney, John J. ed. *Chinese-Western Comparative Literature: Theory and Strategy*. Hong Kong: The Chinese University Press, 1980.

——. "Comparative Literature and China: A Bibliographical Review of Materials in English." *New Asia Academic Bulletin*, Vol. 1, 1978: pp. 287–301.

Donne, John. *Poetical Works*. Ed. by Sir Herbert Grierson. London: Oxford University Press, 1933.

Drayton, Michael. *Minor Poems of Michael Drayton*. Chosen and edited by Cyril Brett. London: Oxford University Press, 1907.

Du Bellay, Joachim. *Les Antiquitez de Rome et Les Regrets*. With an introduction by E. Droz. Genève: Librairie Droz, 1947.

——. *Oeuvres complètes*. Ed. by Léon Séché. Paris: Revue de la Renaissance, 1904–13. 4 Vols.

Fei Sheng-ling. "One Generation of Chinese Studies in Cambridge: An Appreciation of Professor H. A. Giles." *Chinese Social and Political Science Review*, XV, 1931: pp. 79–89.

Fokkema, Douwe W. "New Strategies in the Comparative Study of Literature and Their Application to Contemporary Chinese Literature." *New Asia Academic Bulletin*, Vol. 1, 1978: pp. 1–8.

Fowlie, Wallace. *Mallarmé*. Chicago: Chicago University Press, 1953.

Franke, Herbert. *Sinology at German Universities: with a Supplement on Manchu Studies*. Wiesbaden: Franz Steiner, 1968.

Friedrich, Hugo. *The Structure of Modern Poetry: From the Mid-Nineteenth to the Mid-Twentieth Century*. Tr. by Joachim Neugroschel. Evanston, Illinois: Northwestern University Press, 1974.

Gadamer, Hans-Georg. *Poetica: Ausgewählte Essays*. Frankfurt: Insel Verlag, 1977.

Gardner, Helen ed. *John Donne: A Collection of Critical Essays*. Englewood Cliffs, New Jersey: Prentice-Hall, 1962.

Giles, Herbert. *A History of Chinese Literature*. Rutland, Vermont: Charles E. Tuttle, 1901. Reprint, 1973.

Gilman, Margaret. *The Idea of Poetry in France: From Houdar de la Motte to Baudelaire*. Cambridge, Massachusetts: Harvard University Press, 1958.

Gras, Vernon ed. with Introduction. *European Literary Theory and Practice: From Existential Phenomenology to Structuralism*. New

York: Dell, 1973.

Grube, G. M. A. *A Greek Critic: Demetrius on Style*. Toronto: University of Toronto Press, 1961.

Hamburger, Michael. *Contraries: Studies in German Literature*. New York: Dutton, 1970.

Harding, D. W. "Shelley's Poetry." Boris Ford ed. *The Pelican Guide to English Literature, V: From Blake to Byron*. Harmondsworth, Middlesex: Penguin Books, 1962: pp. 207–19.

Hawkes, David. *A Little Primer of Tu Fu*. London: Oxford University Press, 1967.

——. *Chinese: Classic, Modern, and Humane (An Inaugural Lecture delivered before the University of Oxford on 25 May 1961)*. London: Oxford University Press, 1961.

Hightower, James Robert. *Topics in Chinese Literature: Outlines and Bibliographies*. *Harvard-Yenching Institute Studies* Vol. III. Cambridge, Massachusetts: Harvard University Press, 1950.

Hoffman, Herbert H. ed. *Hoffman's Index to Poetry: European and Latin American Poetry in Anthologies*. Metuchen, New Jersey: Scarecrow, 1985.

Hölderlin, Johann Christian Friedrich. *Sämtliche Werke*. Grosse Stuttgarter Ausgabe. Vols. 1–5: Ed. by Friedrich Beissner. Vols. 6–7: Ed. by Adolf Beck. Stuttgart: Kohlhammer Cotta, 1943–77.

——. *Friedrich Hölderlin: Hymns and Fragments*. Tr. and with an Introduction by Richard Sieburth. Princeton: Princeton University Press, 1984.

Holroyd, Michael. *Lytton Strachey: A Critical Biography*. London: Heinemann, 1967. 2 Vols.

Hosek, Chaviva and Parker, Patricia eds. *Lyric Poetry: Beyond New Criticism*. Ithaca, New York: Cornell University Press, 1985.

Hu Shih. "The Indianization of China: A Case Study in Cultural Borrowing." *Independence, Convergence, and Borrowing in Institutions, Thought, and Art*. *Harvard Tercentenary Publications*. Cambridge, Massachusetts: Harvard University Press, 1937: pp. 219–47.

Huang Yung-wu, "Four Symbolic Plants in Chinese Poetry." Tr. by Wong Wai-leung. *Renditions: A Chinese-English Translation Magazine*, No. 9 (Spring, 1978): pp. 71–80.

Hucker, Charles O. *A Dictionary of Official Titles in Imperial China*. Stanford: Stanford University Press, 1985.

Hult, David ed. *Concepts of Closure. Yale French Studies, 67.* New Haven: Yale University Press, 1984.

Hung, William. *Tu Fu: China's Greatest Poet.* With a Supplementary Volume of Notes. Cambridge, Massachusetts: Harvard University Press, 1952.

Jobes, Gertrude. *Dictionary of Mythology, Folklore and Symbols.* New York: Scarecrow, 1962. 2 Vols.

Johns, Francis A. *A Bibliography of Arthur Waley.* New Brunswick, New Jersey: Rutgers University Press, 1968.

Kao, Yu-kung. "The Aesthetics of regulated Verse." Shuen-fu Lin and Stephen Owen eds. *The Vitality of the Lyric Voice:* Shih *Poetry from the Late Han to the T'ang.* Princeton: Princeton University Press, 1986: pp. 332–85.

—— and Mei, Tsu-lin. "Ending Lines in Wang Shih-chen's 'Ch'i-Chüeh': Convention and Creativity in the Ch'ing." Christian F. Murck ed. *Artists and Traditions.* Princeton: Princeton University Press, 1976: pp. 131–44.

Karlgren, Bernhard. *The Book of Odes: Chinese Text, Transcription and Translation.* Stockholm: The Museum of Far Eastern Antiquities, 1974.

Kennedy, X. J. *An Introduction to Poetry.* Third Edition. Boston: Little, Brown, 1974.

King-hele, Desmond. *Shelley: His Thoughts and Work.* London: Macmillan, 1960.

Lach, Donald F. *China in the Eyes of Europe: The Sixteenth Century.* Chicago: University of Chicago Press, 1965.

Lemon, Lee T. and Reis, Marion J. tr. and with an Introduction. *Russian Formalism Criticism: Four Essays.* Lincoln: University of Nebraska Press, 1965.

Levy, Dore. *Chinese Narrative Poetry.* Durham: Duke University Press, 1988.

Lewis, Roy. *On Reading French Verse: A Study of Poetic Form.* London: Oxford University Press, 1982.

Lin, Shuen-fu. *The Transformation of the Chinese Lyrical Tradition: Chiang K'uei and Southern Sung Tz'u Poetry.* Princeton: Princeton University Press, 1978.

—— and Owen, Stephen eds. *The Vitality of the Lyric Voice: Shih Poetry from the Late Han to T'ang.* Princeton: Princeton University Press, 1986.

Liu, James J. Y. *The Art of Chinese Poetry*. Chicago: University of Chicago Press, 1962.

——. *Chinese Theories of Literature*. Chicago: University of Chicago Press, 1975.

——. *The Interlingual Critic: Interpreting Chinese Poetry*. Bloomington: Indiana University Press, 1982.

——. *Language—Paradox—Poetics: A Chinese Perspective*. Princeton: Princeton University Press, 1988.

Longfellow, Henry Wadsworth. *The Poetical Works of Longfellow*. Cambridge Edition. With a New Introduction by George Monteiro. Boston: Houghton Mifflin, 1975.

Lynn, Richard John. *Chinese Literature: A Draft Bibliography in West European Languages. Oriental Monograph Series No. 24*. Canberra: Australian National University Press, 1979.

Mallarmé, Stéphane. *Oeuvres complètes de Stéphane Mallarmé*. Ed. and annotated by Henri Mondor and G. Jean-Aubry. Paris: Gallimard, 1945.

Mason, Mary Gertrude. *Western Concepts of China and the Chinese, 1840–1876*. New York, 1939.

Matejka, Ladislav and Pomorska, Krystyna eds. *Readings in Russian Poetics: Formalist and Structuralist Views*. Ann Arbor: University of Michigan Press, 1978.

McCraw, David R. *Du Fu's Laments from the South*. Honolulu: University of Hawaii Press, 1992.

Medhurst, W. H. "Chinese Poetry: A Lecture Delivered at Shanghai." *The China Review*, Vol. IV, July and August 1875: pp. 46–56.

Miner, Earl. "Pound, Haiku, and the Image." Walter Sutton ed. *Ezra Pound: A Collection of Critical Essays*. Englewood Cliffs, New Jersey: Prentice-Hall, 1963: pp. 115–28.

Morris, Ivan ed. *Madly Singing in the Mountains: An Appreciation and Anthology of Arthur Waley*. New York: Walker, 1970.

Musser, Frederic O. *Strange Clamor: A Guide to the Critical Reading of French Poetry*. Detroit: Wayne State University Press, 1965.

Nerval, Gérard de. *Oeuvres*. Ed. and annotated by Albert Béguin and Jean Richer. Paris: Gallimard, 1966. 2 Vols.

Nienhauser, William H. Jr. ed. *The Indiana Companion to Traditional Chinese Literature*. Bloomington: Indiana University Press, 1986.

The Norton Anthology of Poetry. Ed. by Alexander W. Allison et als. Third Edition. New York: W. W. Norton, 1983.

Owen, Stephen. *The Great Age of Chinese Poetry: The High T'ang*. New Haven: Yale University Press, 1981.

——. *Poetry of the Early T'ang*. New Haven: Yale University Press, 1977.

——. *Readings in Chinese Literary Thought*. Cambridge, Massachusetts: Harvard University Press, 1992.

——. *Traditional Chinese Poetry and Poetics: Omen of the World*. Madison: University of Wisconsin Press, 1985.

The Oxford English Dictionary. Second Edition. Prepared by J. A. Simpson and E. S. C. Weiner. Oxford: Clarendon Press, 1989. 20 Vols.

Palumbo-Liu, David. *The Poetics of Appropriation: The Literary Theory and Practice of Huang Tingjian*. Stanford: Stanford University Press, 1993.

Pater, Walter. *Selected Writings of Walter Pater*. Ed. by Harold Bloom. New York: Signet, 1974.

Plato. *Phaedo*. Tr. by Benjamin Jowett. Charles M. Eliot ed. *Plato, Epictetus, Marcus Aurelius. The Harvard Classics*. Danbury, Connecticut: Grolier, 1907, 1980: pp. 45–113.

Pound, Ezra. *The Classic Anthology defined by Confucius*. Cambridge, Massachusetts: Harvard University Press, 1954.

Princeton Encyclopedia of Poetry and Poetics. Ed. by Alex Preminger. Enlarged Edition. Princeton: Princeton University Press, 1974.

Purcell, V. W. W. S. *The Spirit of Chinese Poetry: An Original Essay*. Singapore: Kelly & Walsh, 1929.

Reichwein, Adolf. *China und Europa: Geistige und Künstlerische Beziehungen im 18. Jahrhundert*. Berlin: Oesterheld, 1923.

Richards, I. A. *Practical Criticism: A Study of Literary Judgment*. New York: Harcourt, Brace World, 1929, Harvest Book, 1956.

——. *Principles of Literary Criticism*. New York: Harcourt Brace Jovanovich, 1925.

Rickett, Adele Austin ed. *Chinese Approaches to Literature from Confucius to Liang Ch'i-ch'ao*. Princeton: Princeton University Press, 1978.

Rimbaud, Arthur. *Oeuvres complètes*. Ed. and annotated by Antoine Adam. Paris: Gallimard, 1972.

Russell, R.A. and Winterbottom, M. ed. *Ancient Literary Criticism: The Principle Texts in New Translations*. London: Oxford University Press, 1972.

Ryan, Thomas E. *Hölderlin's Silence*. New York: Peter Lang, 1988.

Sainte-Beuve, Charles-Augustin de. *Tableau historique et critique de la poésie française et du théâtre français au seizième siècle*. Paris: Charpentier, 1969.

Santner, Eric L. *Friedrich Hölderlin: Narrative Vigilance and the Poetic Imagination*. New Brunswick, New Jersey: Rutgers University Press, 1986.

Schuster, Ingrid. *China und Japan in der deutschen Literatur: 1800–1925*. 1977.

Schwartz, William Leonard. *The Imaginative Interpretation of the Far East in Modern French Literature: 1800–1925*. Paris: Librairie ancienne honoré champion, 1927.

Shelley, Percy Bysshe. *The Complete Poetical Works of Percy Bysshe Shelley*. Ed. by Neville Rogers. London: Oxford University Press. 1972. 4 Vols.

——. *Poetical Works*. Ed. by Thomas Hutchinson. London: Oxford University Press, 1905.

Shklovsky, Viktor. *Theory of Prose*. Tr. by Benjamin Sher with an Introduction by Gerald L. Gruns. Elmwood Park, Illinois: Dalkey Archives Press, 1990.

Sidney, Sir Philip. *The Poems of Sir Philip Sidney*. Ed. by William A. Ringler, Jr. London: Oxford University Press, 1962.

Smith, Barbara Herrnstein. *Poetic Closure: A Study of How Poems End*. Chicago: University of Chicago Press, 1968.

Soong, Stephen C. ed. *A Brotherhood in Song: Chinese Poetry and Poetics*. Hong Kong: Chinese University Press, 1985.

Steiner, George. *After Babel: Aspects of Language and Translation*. London: Oxford University Press, 1975.

——. *Language and Silence: Essays on Language, Literature, and the Inhuman*. New York: Atheneum, 1977.

Strachey, Lytton. "An Anthology." *New Quarterly* I (October 1908): pp. 603–10.

——. "Modern Poetry." *Spectator*, 100, April 18, 1908: pp. 622–23.

Taupin, René. *L'Influence du symbolisme français sur la poésie américaine de 1910 à 1920*. Genève: Slatkine, 1975.

Tay, William. "The Substantive Level Revisited: Concreteness and Nature Imagery in T'ang Poetry." *New Asia Academic Bulletin*, Vol. 1, 1978: pp. 127–49.

Teele, Roy Earl. *Through a Glass Darkly: A Study of English*

Translations of Chinese Poetry. Ph.D. dissertation, Columbia University. Ann Arbor, Michigan, 1949.

Tompkins, Jane P. ed. *Reader-Response Criticism: From Formalism to Post-Structuralism*. Baltimore, Maryland: Johns Hopkins University Press, 1980.

Van Zoeren, Steven. *Poetry and Personality: Reading, Exegesis, and Hermeneutics in Traditional China*. Stanford: Stanford University Press, 1991.

Vendler, Helen. *The Music of What Happens: Poems, Poets, Critics*. Cambridge, Massachusetts: Harvard University Press, 1988.

Villon, François. *Poésies*. Ed. by Jean Dufournet with a Preface by Tristan Tzara. Paris: Gallimard, 1973.

Virgil. *The Aeneid*. Ed. with Introduction and Commentary by J. W. Mackail. London: Oxford University Press, 1930.

——. *The Aeneid*. Tr. by Robert Fitzgerald. New York: Random House, 1983.

Von Zach, Erwin tr. *Tu Fu's Gedichte*. Ed. and with an Introduction by James Robert Hightower. *Harvard-Yenching Institute Studies VIII*. Cambridge, Massachusetts: Harvard University Press, 1952.

Waley, Arthur tr. *A Hundred and Seventy Chinese Poems*. London: Constable, 1918.

—— tr. *The Book of Songs: Translated from the Chinese*. New Foreword by Stephen Owen. New York: Grove Press, 1987.

——. "Our Debt to China." *Asiatic Review*, XXXVI, July 1940: p. 554.

—— tr. *The Temple and Other Poems*. New York: Alfred A. Knopf, 1923.

Wang, C. H. *The Bell and the Drum: Shih Ching as Formulaic Poetry in an Oral Tradition*. Berkeley: University of California Press, 1974.

Watson, Burton. *Chinese Lyricism: Shih Poetry from the Second to the Twelfth Century with Translations*. New York: Columbia University Press, 1971.

——. *Early Chinese Literature*. New York: Columbia University Press, 1962.

Wellek, René and Warren, Austin. *Theory of Literature*. Third Edition. Harmondsworth, Middlesex: Penguin Books, 1963.

White, T. H. tr. and ed. *The Bestiary: A Book of Beasts*. New York: Capricorn, 1960.

Whitman, Walt. *The Complete Poetry and Prose of Walt Whitman*. With an Introduction by Malcolm Cowley. New York: Pelligrini and

Cadahy, 1948. 2 Vols.

Wong, Siu-kit ed. and tr. *Early Chinese Literary Criticism*. With a Preface by David Hawkes. Hong Kong: Joint Publishing Co., 1983.

Woolf, Virginia. "Mr. Bennett and Mrs. Brown." From Robert Scholes ed. *Approaches to the Novel: Materials for a Poetics*. San Francisco: Chandler, 1961: pp. 211-30.

Wordsworth, Dorothy. *Journals of Dorothy Wordsworth: The Alfoxden Journal, 1798* [and] *The Grasmere Journals, 1800-1803*. With an Appendix of Wordsworth's Shorter Poems Referred to in the Journals. Ed. and with an Introduction by Helen Darbishire. London: Oxford University Press, 1963.

Wordsworth, William. *The Poetical Works of William Wordsworth*. Ed. by E. de Selincourt. Second Edition. London: Oxford University Press, 1952. 4 Vols.

Yip, Wai-lim ed. and tr. *Chinese Poetry: Major Modes and Genres*. Berkeley: University of California Press, 1976.

——. *Ezra Pound's Cathay*. Princeton: Princeton University Press, 1969.

Yu, Pauline. *The Poetry of Wang Wei: New Translations and Commentary*. Bloomington: Indiana University Press, 1980.

——. *The Reading of Imagery in the Chinese Tradition*. Princeton: Princeton University Press, 1987.

Index

ASIAN THOUGHT AND CULTURE

This series is designed to cover three inter-related projects:

- *Asian Classics Translation*, including those modern Asian works that have been generally accepted as "classics"
- *Asian and Comparative Philosophy and Religion*, including excellent and publishable Ph.D. dissertations, scholarly monographs, or collected essays
- *Asian Thought and Culture in a Broader Perspective*, covering exciting and publishable works in Asian culture, history, political and social thought, education, literature, music, fine arts, performing arts, martial arts, medicine, etc.

For additional information about this series or for the submission of manuscripts, please contact:

Peter Lang Publishing, Inc.
Acquisitions Department
29 Broadway, 18th floor
New York, New York 10006

To order other books in this series, please contact our Customer Service Department at:

800-770-LANG (within the U.S.)
(212) 647-7706 (outside the U.S.)
(212) 647-7707 FAX

Or browse online by series at:

www.peterlang.com